# Teach the Bairns Vegetarian Cooking

## Traditional Scottish Recipes for Beginners

Liz Ashworth
Foreword by Nick Nairn

illustrated by children from
Mosstodloch Primary School

SCOTTISH CHILDREN'S PRESS

D0177284

Published in 1999 by

SCOTTISH CHILDREN'S PRESS

Unit 13d, Newbattle Abbey Business Annexe,
Newbattle Road, Dalkeith, EH22 3LJ
Tel: 0131 660 4757 • Fax: 0131 660 6414
Email: scp@sol.co.uk

**British Library Cataloguing in Publication Data**
A catalogue record for this book is available from the British Library

ISBN: 1 899827 66 8

Printed and bound by Cromwell Press, Trowbridge, Wiltshire

**Teach the Bairns Vegetarian Cooking** is the third in
an exciting series of Scottish recipe books for beginners.

Also available:

### Teach the Bairns to Cook
Traditional Scottish Recipes for Beginners

1 899827 23 4

### Teach the Bairns to Bake
Traditional Scottish Baking for Beginners

1 899827 24 2

Look out for further titles in the Children's Cooking
series, including: *Teagaisg Cocaireachd Dhan Chloinne*
(*Teach the Bairns to Cook* in Gaelic)

Please contact **SCOTTISH CHILDREN'S PRESS** for
further details or for a complete catalogue

*Whether therefore ye eat, or drink, or whatsoever ye do, do all to the Glory of God.*
(1 Corinthians 10, Verse 31)

# Contents

# Foreword

In these enlightened times cooking without meat is no longer considered to be an eccentric oddity, and over the last few years vegetarian cooking has even managed to shed completely its bland or 'cranky' image to become trendy. Mouth-watering recipes like Oatmeal Muffins and Red Pottage show just how exciting and appealing this type of cuisine can be. And you don't have to be a vegetarian to enjoy it.

It is a sad fact that at the beginning of the new century we Scots have one of the least healthy diets in Europe despite being surrounded by some of the best quality produce in the world. Vegetarian cooking is not necessarily the 'cure all' for Scottish health, but teaching the bairns to cook is. The secret of the health of the nation lies in nurturing our children's interest in preparing and enjoying food. After all, what could be a better gift for the next generation than giving them the confidence and inspiration to experiment with a wide variety of dishes?

When children learn to cook, they learn to understand a lot more about food. They also experience a certain freedom that comes with the ability to be creative with any ingredients to hand. The only way that anybody learns to cook is by rolling up their sleeves, getting into the kitchen and making dishes that they think are tasty – dishes which inspire them.

A point to bear in mind whether you are a parent who is hoping to guide their kids through vegetarian cooking, or a kid who is hoping to guide their parents through, do try and get the best local ingredients you can. Once you eliminate meat, poultry and fish from the shopping list you have taken off the most expensive items which should mean you have a wee bit of lee-way to get the highest quality ingredients possible. If you are lucky enough to have some space where you can grow some of your own vegetables you will have access to the tastiest raw materials. Similarly, farmers' markets present better quality at a lower price and are great fun to go to if you happen to have one near to you.

At the end of the day the important thing is for everybody to be healthy and happy. Don't be afraid to get the kitchen mucky. Encourage your kids at every chance you get to jump into the kitchen and start experimenting. Remember they will be teaching their own children one day.

Food is far more than mere fuel.
Recipes are a key to freedom, creativity, health and fun.

*Nick Nairn*

# Introduction

The aim of this book is to keep traditional Scottish recipes alive by presenting them in a simple, interesting way, so that 'bairns' will find them easy to prepare and fun to eat. Each recipe is graded simple, intermediate and advanced – it is intended that adults will always supervise children when they are cooking.

In the past, most working Scots could not afford to buy meat so they ate a vegetarian diet based on the fruit and vegetables they cultivated or found growing wild – oatmeal, milk, butter, cheese and eggs. Their diet was wholesome and healthy; free from additives, colourings and preservatives. It is recognised that many of our children's health and behavioural problems are caused by such additions to our modern diet. This book addresses this problem, providing a wide range of interesting recipes which are additive, colouring and preservative free. While adapting the recipes, I have also taken into account 'nut allergy' problems – all the dishes are made with sunflower or olive oil and those which do contain nuts clearly indicate that these may be omitted.

My thanks to Gordon Baxter for his continued support and encouragement; to Nick Nairn who found time in his hectic schedule to write the enthusiastic and exciting foreword; to Janet Hall (a pupil at Elgin Academy) for providing a juggling McChef for the cover; to Mr Corsie, the Headmaster, and the staff and pupils at Mosstodloch Primary School for their artistic contributions.

Use this book to learn and have fun with food – good food is what we need to build a strong body, and we need a healthy body to be active and enjoy life!

*Liz Ashworth*

**Editor's Note:** The recipes have been adapted and approved by qualified dieticians. The more healthy versions of the ingredients have been placed in brackets; this allows you to see and follow the healthy option, but means that you can still make the recipe if you only have the higher fat ingredients. Try to remember when you are buying your ingredients and planning meals that:

- All the milk used is semi-skimmed.
- Use half-fat cheddar, gouda or edam cheese.
- The jam used is reduced-sugar, high-fruit.
- For a healthier diet, try not to eat more than two eggs a week.

# Important: Before You Begin to Cook

1) **Always** ask an adult for permission before you cook. If you are unsure or have never cooked on your own before do not be embarrassed to ask for help.

2) Decide on the recipe you would like to make and check how long it will take. Always read the recipe carefully right through before you start. Make sure you understand everything you have to do. Read through the list of ingredients and utensils again and set out everything you will need on the table before you start preparing the dish.

3) Arrange the shelves in the oven to the position indicated in the recipe before you turn on the oven to heat at the required temperature. (When you are using the oven, it is more economical to plan ahead and make a few things at the same time. Cook the recipe which needs the hottest temperature first.)

4) Always use a chopping board to chop food. Never hold a knife by its blade.

5) Have a heat-resistant surface nearby to set hot tins and baking trays on. A wooden chopping board will do.

6) A minute timer will make sure that the timing of your recipes is accurate. It will help you to remember your cooking while you are tidying up afterwards!

7) Weigh all the ingredients very carefully – this is very important. If you do not have kitchen scales, you can buy inexpensive measuring spoons and scoops from hardware shops which will help you to measure the quantities easily and accurately.

8) Wash and dry your hands, and all work surfaces, before you start.

9) For safety in the kitchen:
   - Tie back long hair.
   - Wear an apron or overall.
   - Do not wear open shoes or sandals in case of spills.
   - When you are stirring, mixing or beating, put a clean, damp cloth under the bowl to stop it from slipping.
   - Use oven gloves or mitts on both hands to lift hot trays, dishes, tins or pans.
   - Be careful with pans and girdles on the hob. Turn the handles inwards so that they can't be knocked off the hob. Be careful that handles do not overhang the hot hob. Always hold the handle of a pan when you are stirring or turning food.

10) Remember to turn off the oven, hob, gas or electricity when you have finished using it.

# Oven Temperatures and Safety Tips

## Your Oven

Check whether your oven is gas or electric. An electric oven can be measured in two ways:

- If your oven shows a temperature range from 0° to 550°, it is measured in degrees Fahrenheit.
- If it shows a range from 0° to 250°, it is measured in degrees Celsius.

The temperature of a fan oven is higher than that of a conventional oven. You will need to decrease the baking temperature according to the manufacturer's instructions.

**Be sure to read the recipe carefully and set your oven to the correct temperature.**

Gas Mark

| | | | |
|---|---|---|---|
| 1 | 275°F | 140°C | low |
| 2 | 300°F | 150°C | |
| 3 | 325°F | 170°C | moderately low |
| 4 | 350°F | 180°C | moderate |
| 5 | 375°F | 190°C | |
| 6 | 400°F | 200°C | moderately hot |
| 7 | 425°F | 220°C | hot |
| 8 | 450°F | 230°C | very hot |
| 9 | 475°F | 240°C | |

## Oven shelves

Different recipes are baked in different parts of the oven. Arrange the shelves for the recipe **before** you turn on the oven. If you need to re-arrange the shelves, use oven gloves.

## If you burn yourself

- Call for an adult to come and help.
- If your skin is splashed with a hot liquid, or is touched by steam, or you accidentally touch a hot surface, put the affected area under cold running water as quickly as you can. This will take the heat out of the burn. You should keep it in the cold water for about 10 minutes.
- Remember, the quicker you get the burn into cold water the better chance you have of stopping it from blistering and causing scarring.
- You should be very careful around steam and boiling fat or oil. Steam and cooking fat are very hot, hotter than boiling water, and can give you a very nasty burn.

## In Case of Fire

- Call an adult.
- Turn off the heat if it is **safe** to do so.
- Get away from the fire.
- Do NOT put water on it.

# Simple Spoonfuls

### 'level' and 'rounded'

Take a knife and smooth the amount on the top of the spoon so that it is flat – this is called a 'level spoonful', sometimes called a 'half spoonful'.

One level teaspoon = half a teaspoon

One level tablespoon = ½ oz = 12.5g

When an amount of, say, flour is described as 'rounded', there is as much flour on the top of the spoon as the shape of the spoon below.

One rounded teaspoon = 1 teaspoonful

One rounded tablespoon of flour = 1oz = 25g

One tablespoon of liquid = 1 fl.oz = 25ml

## dessertspoon

A dessertspoon is a spoon which is bigger than a teaspoon but smaller than a tablespoon.

One rounded tablespoon = 1oz

One rounded dessertspoon = ½ oz

One rounded teaspoon = ¼ oz

# Easy Eggs

### breaking eggs

Never break an egg directly into food in case it is bad. Hold the egg over a cup and tap the middle of the shell with a knife to crack it. Carefully open the shell with your thumbs and let the inside of the egg drop into the cup. Check its smell and colour to see if the egg is fresh. If the recipe needs more than one egg, always break them into a cup one at a time and then add to a bowl for mixing. This means that you can throw out one which may not be fresh before it is mixed with the others.

### Two ways to separate egg yolk and white

1  **Use an egg separator:** an egg separator is like a small round flat cup with a slit in the side of it. Hold it over a bowl and break the egg into the cup; the egg white will run out of the slit into the bowl, leaving the egg yolk in the cup.

2  **Use the eggshell:** wash and dry the egg very carefully. Break the egg into a cup or bowl. Take half of the clean eggshell and carefully cut into the egg white with the sharp shell and lift out the yolk. Eggshell is more effective than a spoon because the sharpness of the shell cuts away the white sticking to the yolk and makes it easier to lift out. It is also perfect for lifting out any small broken pieces of eggshell.

 # Preparing Vegetables

## beetroot

Beetroot is a root vegetable with bright pink flesh. Wear rubber gloves to peel beetroot – cooked or raw – and keep the beetroot separate from other food, otherwise you will find that your hands and food turn pink too!

## cabbage, kail, etc. (green vegetables)

Prepare green vegetables just before you cook them so that they keep their nutrients. Cut off the root, peel off any dead or tough outer leaves and throw them away. Wash under cold running water and drain in a colander. Place on a chopping board and use a sharp knife to cut off and throw away any thick stalks or stringy parts. Cut into thin strips (called 'shreds') or large pieces according to the recipe.

## cauliflower and broccoli

Remove the outer leaves and cut away the thick stem – throw these away. Wash the vegetable under cold running water, place on a chopping board and cut the flower into smaller, even-sized flowers – called 'sprigs'. Place the sprigs in a clean pan or bowl and cover with cold water until you are ready to cook them. Just before cooking, drain off the water through a colander placed in the sink, and boil in fresh, salted water for about 8 minutes until tender.

## leeks and spring onions

Place the leeks or spring onions on a chopping board and use a sharp knife to cut off the root and remove any dead outer leaves. Trim off the tops and throw these away too. Wash under cold running water. **Leeks:** Cut the leeks in half lengthways and run the water inside to wash out any soil. **Spring Onions:** Cut the stalks with a pair of scissors. Leeks and spring onions can be cut into **different shapes**:

**Rings:** lay the stalks on a chopping board and cut across the length of the vegetable to make small rings.

**Dice:** lay the stalks on the chopping board and cut along the length of the stalks to make strips, then cut across these to make small squares, also called 'dice'.

## onions

Place the onion on a chopping board and use a sharp knife to cut off the root and stalk ends. Remove the papery outer skin. **To slice the onion:** cut it in half from top to bottom. Lay one half of the onion on its flat side. Hold it with one hand and cut it into thin slices from top to bottom. Do the same with the other half. **To chop the onion:** slice the onion (see above) then cut across the slices to make small squares. A friend of mine wears swimming goggles while doing this to stop her from crying!

9

## potatoes, carrots, parsnips

Wash the vegetables under cold running water. Use a potato peeler or a sharp knife to peel off a thin skin. Cut out and throw away any bruised, discoloured or rotten pieces using the point of the knife or peeler. Cut into even sizes on a chopping board with a sharp knife. Place the pieces in a pan or bowl and cover with cold water until you are ready to use them.

## boiling potatoes, carrots, parsnips

Drain any water used to soak the vegetables by tipping them into a colander in the sink. Place the vegetables in a pan and cover with boiling water. Add a pinch of salt (2 level teaspoons for potatoes) and bring to the boil on a medium to high heat. Reduce the heat until the vegetables are simmering, put the lid on the pan and cook until tender (20 minutes for potatoes). Test by sticking a knife into the vegetables: if it goes in easily, they are cooked. Place a colander in the sink. Using oven gloves, carefully lift the pan, remove the lid and tip the vegetables and water into the colander to drain. Be careful to keep your face away from the hot steam which could burn you – another trick is to run cold water into the sink to help stop the steam from filling the kitchen.

## tomatoes

Wash and dry tomatoes, and remove the green stalk. Place the tomatoes on a chopping board and use a sharp knife to slice each tomato in half from top (stalk end) to bottom. Cut a little 'v' shape round the hard piece of stalk on each half of the tomato, remove it and throw it away. **To make slices:** lay the tomato on its flat side and holding it steady with one hand cut into slices across the tomato. **To dice the tomato:** cut across the slices to make little squares. **To quarter for salads:** cut in half through the stalk, cut out the little 'v' shape then cut each piece of tomato in half again.

## turnips and swedes

Turnips and swedes have a thick skin. Peel it off with a sharp knife. Cut out and throw away any bruised, discoloured or rotten pieces. Cut into even sizes on a chopping board with a sharp knife. Place the pieces in a bowl or pan and cover with water until you are ready to use them.

## testing cooked vegetables

Use the point of a sharp knife or skewer to test that vegetables are cooked. Push the point into the flesh and if it goes all the way through easily, the vegetables are cooked.

# Preparing Fruit and Herbs

## apples and pears

Wash under cold running water. Remove the skin with a potato peeler. Place on a chopping board and slice the fruit in half from top (stalk end) to bottom. Lay on its flat side and cut in half again. Remove the core from each quarter with a sharp knife. Use as soon as possible – if you have to leave the fruit, place in a bowl and cover with cold water. Add a little lemon juice to prevent the fruit going brown.

## gooseberries, black and redcurrants

Use a pair of scissors to cut off the stalk and dry leafy part at the opposite end. This is called 'topping and tailing'. Place in a sieve or colander and wash under cold running water. Drain and use.

## raspberries and blackberries

Remove the leaves and white inner core using your thumb and forefinger. Put into a colander and wash quickly but gently (so as not to bruise the fruit) under cold running water. Drain and use.

## rhubarb

Place on a chopping board and use a sharp knife to remove the leaves and bottom of the stem. Wash under cold running water and dry with a clean tea towel. Cut across the stalks to the size you need on a clean chopping board.

## strawberries

Remove the leaves and white core using a pair of sugar tongs or tweezers. Put into a colander and wash under cold running water. Drain and use.

## testing cooked fruit

Use the point of a sharp knife or skewer to test that fruit is cooked. Push the point into the flesh and if it goes all the way through easily, the fruit is cooked.

## herbs

Wash under cold running water, drain well in a colander or sieve, and dry thoroughly in a clean tea towel or kitchen towel. Remove the tough stalks with a pair of kitchen scissors and cut into small pieces. (This is easier and safer than chopping small sprigs with a sharp knife.)

**Dried herbs** can be used instead of fresh herbs. Use half the quantity of dried herbs compared with fresh herbs.

# Handy Hints

### covering a bowl to steam

Measure across the top of the bowl, add 15cm (6 inches) and cut a square of aluminium foil to this measurement. Make a little tuck in the middle of the square about 1cm (½ inch) wide (this is to allow the food in the bowl to rise as it cooks). Cover the bowl with foil and tie securely round the top of the bowl with string or a thick elastic band.

### a 'double boiler'

A double boiler is two pans in one! The outer pan is filled with hot water and the inner container holds the mixture (for example, chocolate) you wish to cook, melt or soften.

### testing the temperature of fat or oil

Drop in a piece of dry bread to test the temperature of hot fat or oil (stand back so that the oil does not splash and burn you). If the bread bubbles and turns golden, the fat or oil is ready. If the bread burns, the fat is too hot. If the fat does not bubble it is too cold.

### pan sizes

**saucepan** – holds 1½–2 pints (1.25 litres) of water
**stew pan** – holds 3–4 pints (2.5 litres) of water
**large soup pot** – holds 5–6 pints (3.5 litres) of water

# Key

| | |
|---|---|
| Simple | Simple, straightforward recipe |
| Inter | Will require some help |
| Adv | Will need supervision and help throughout this recipe |
| 1 hr 20 mins | The recipe will take one hour and 20 minutes to make (this time will change for each recipe) |
| Cook ≋ | Needs cooking |
| No Cook ☒ | No cooking required |
| Hob ◎ | Uses the hob |
| Grill ⌘ | Uses the grill |
| Girdle ♉ | A girdle may be used |
| E. Wok ◐ | An electric wok may be used |
| E. Fry ❖ | An electric frying pan may be used |
| Oven ☐ | Uses the oven |
| Freeze ✳ | Recipe may be frozen |

# Simple Cooking Terms

**Batter**  A mix of flour, eggs and liquid. The thickness of the batter depends on what it is to be used to make. A batter which will coat the food is the thickness of double cream.

**Beat**  To stir food fast. You can use a spoon, whisk or electric beater.

**Blend**  To use a liquidiser, blender or sieve and spoon to make something smooth in consistency and remove all the lumps (for example, in soups and sauces).

**Boil**  To cook food over a high heat so that the liquid moves; bubbles appear and steam rises from it.

**Chop**  To cut food into small pieces. To chop something finely is to cut it up as small as you can.

**Dough**  Dough is a mixture of flour (or meal) and a liquid. It is stiff and elastic like play dough. The stiffness depends on the food you are making.

**Egg wash**  Also called 'egg glaze'. To paint the top of dough or pastry with beaten egg to give a golden shiny top when baked.

**Dice**  To cut food into small equal sized cubes.

**Drain**  To pour off the liquid which you don't need. You usually use a colander or a sieve which is placed over the sink or (if you need to save the liquid) a bowl.

**Folding in**  To very gently mix two or more ingredients together. Using a tablespoon the mixture is lifted and mixed with light strokes. This mixing method is used so that the air in the mixture is not knocked out by stirring too much.

**Grate**  To rub food against a grater so that it is made into crumbs or fine shreds. To grate citrus rind, wash the fruit well, put the grater on a plate and rub the skin on the rough dimpled part of the grater until you have rubbed off the coloured waxy outer surface of the skin – do not rub into the white part called 'pith' which has a bitter taste. Use a knife to scrape all the peel off the grater.

**Grease**  To rub something, for example a baking dish or tray, with butter, margarine or oil. This stops the food from sticking to it.

**Knead**  To mix dough together using both hands. On a floured surface, push the dough down and away from you while squeezing it together. Still squeezing, pull the dough back towards you, then push it down and away again. Do this until the dough is smooth and mixed.

**Marinate**  To soak food in a mixture called a 'marinade' which will add flavour and tenderise the food before cooking.

| | |
|---|---|
| **Pinch** | A pinch is the amount you can hold between your thumb and forefinger (pointing finger). |
| **Shred** | To cut food, for example cabbage, into very thin small strips. |
| **Sieve** | To rub flour and other dry ingredients through a sieve placed over a mixing bowl. Use the back of a tablespoon to push everything through the sieve. This removes any lumps or dirt and adds air to your baking. |
| **Simmer** | To cook food over a low heat so that it bubbles now and again. |
| **Slice** | To cut food into thin portions. |
| **Soak** | To cover an ingredient with a liquid (usually water, fruit juices or milk) and leave for a period of time (overnight or a few hours). Food is soaked to soften it, to remove impurities or to allow the liquid to be absorbed. |
| **Stir** | To mix ingredients together with a spoon or fork until they are all well blended together. |
| **Sweating** | To cook very slowly in a little oil, margarine or butter until soft. |
| **Tasting** | To eat a tiny amount of the food you are cooking to check the seasoning or sweetness so that you can add salt, pepper, spices or sugar as required to make the flavour better. Dip a spoon into the food you are tasting and drop some on to your spoon. Never put the spoon which has been in your mouth back into the food. |
| **Water Bath** | To cook food in a dish or tin which is half filled with warm water and placed in the oven. This is used to cook very delicate foods such as egg custards which need to cook slowly and gently. |
| **Whip** | To beat a liquid with a whisk. Egg whites will become light and frothy do not overbeat them or they will become liquid again. Cream will become fluffy, thicker and increased in volume. Take care not to overbeat or it will become butter. |

# Soup

Traditional Highland cottages consisted of two rooms, called the 'but and ben'. The family lived, ate and slept in the larger part called the 'but'. There was a peat fire in the middle of this room, over which hung a large black iron pot. All the family's meals were cooked in this pot. There was a hole in the roof to allow the smoke to escape. Since the hole let in rain as well as letting the smoke out, it could not be directly over the fire as the rain would put the fire out! So very little of the smoke actually found its way out of the cottage; instead it filled the room and billowed out of the door. The Scottish housewife was not hindered by the lack of kitchen facilities. The great iron pot produced plenty of wholesome food for the family like filling, nourishing soups. The main vegetables in these soups were kail and cabbage – common in many Highland gardens – and so the Highlander's vegetable patch became known as his 'kailyard'. Because kail was used so much in their food, the Scots began to refer to their main meal as their 'kail' and the pot in which it was cooked as the 'kail pot'.

# Green Kail, also called Pan Kail

*An old Scottish song says: 'The Friars of Faill, they made gude kail'*
*(Faill was a monastery in Ayrshire where the food must have been very good!).*

Inter

Serves 4–6

1 hr 15 mins

Cook ≈

Hob ◎

E. Wok ○

E. Fry ❖

No Freeze

16

## Have Ready

450g (1lb) 'greens' (curly kail, Savoy cabbage, spinach)

2 level tablespoons medium oatmeal

2 tablespoons cream (single or half-fat)

1 level teaspoon salt

1 litre (1½ pints) water

large soup pot

hand blender or liquidiser

large bowl

pair of kitchen scissors

measuring jug

colander or large sieve

draining spoon

wooden spoon

tablespoon

teaspoon

oven gloves

## To Make

1 Prepare the green vegetables: wash each leaf well in running cold water. Drain well in a sieve or colander. Hold the leaves over a bowl and use a pair of kitchen scissors to cut them roughly into smaller pieces.

2 Pour the water into the pan and place it on the hob. Turn the heat to high. When the water is boiling, carefully add the 'greens' (wear oven gloves to protect your hands from the steam). Use the wooden spoon to push the greens into the water.

3 Bring to the boil and reduce the heat until the greens are simmering. Cook for 45 minutes checking every 15 minutes to make sure there is enough water to cover the greens: add a little more water if you think it is needed.

4 Turn off the heat and set the pan on a heat-resistant surface for 10 minutes to cool.

5 Use the blender or liquidiser to blend the greens and water into a smooth soup. (If you do not have a blender, use a draining spoon to lift the greens on to a plate. Carefully chop them into small pieces with a knife and fork and use the draining spoon to put them back in the pan.)

6  Sprinkle the oatmeal over the soup, add the salt and pepper and stir well.

7  Place the pan back on the heat and stir in the cream. Heat until boiling and boil for 2 minutes.

8  Carefully dip in a tablespoon and drop some of the soup on to a teaspoon. Wait until it has cooled before you taste it. Add more salt and pepper if you think it needs it.

9  Serve hot in deep soup bowls with crisp, thin oatcakes. One of the tastiest ways to 'eat up your greens'!

# Oatmeal Soup

The 'corn lands' (the ground used to grow oats and barley) of the Highlands of Scotland were mostly shallow, rocky ground. The soil was cultivated with what was called a 'crooked spade', which was a narrow blade of iron attached to a long, heavy piece of wood with a handle just above the blade. The 'crooked spade' was used as a spade to till the ground, and as a lever to remove large stones in the rocky soil.

Inter

Serves 3

1 hr 30 mins

Cook ≋

Hob ◎

E. Wok ◯

E. Fry ❖

18

## HAVE READY

1 large onion – peeled, chopped

1 carrot – peeled, chopped

¼ turnip – peeled, chopped

1 leek – finely chopped

25g (1oz) medium oatmeal

1 vegetable stock cube

425ml (¾ pint) milk (semi-skimmed)

570ml (1 pint) boiling water

1 dessertspoon olive oil

1 tablespoon chopped parsley

1 level teaspoon salt

pinch pepper

large soup pot + lid

heat-proof measuring jug

wooden spoon

tablespoon

dessertspoon

teaspoon

saucer or spoon rest

oven gloves

## TO MAKE

1 Prepare the vegetables (see pages 9 and 10).

2 Pour the olive oil into the soup pot and put on a medium heat.

3 Heat the oil for a minute and add a piece of onion. When it starts to sizzle, add all the vegetables and stir well with the wooden spoon until they are coated in oil. Cook the vegetables for 2 to 3 minutes, stirring all the time, until the onion and leek become clear – this is called 'sweating' the vegetables.

4 Turn the heat to low, remove the wooden spoon and put the lid on the pot. Cook for 5 minutes.

5 Use the oven gloves to lift the lid off the pot, watching out for the hot steam which will escape. Add the oatmeal to the soup pot and cook for 2 minutes, stirring well with the wooden spoon.

6 Put the stock cube in the jug. Carefully pour in the boiling water until it comes up to the 570ml (1 pint) mark and stir with the wooden spoon until the stock cube dissolves.

7 Turn up the heat to medium, add the stock and stir with the wooden spoon until the soup boils.

8 Reduce the heat until the soup is just moving in the pot (this is called 'simmering'). Put on the lid and cook for 45 minutes.

9 Use the oven gloves to lift the lid and add the salt, pepper and chopped parsley.

10 Add the milk just before serving the soup, bring to the boil again and serve at once. I think you will enjoy this soup – and oatmeal is very good for you.

# Red Pottage

Lady Elizabeth Grant of Rothiemurchus, or the 'Highland Lady' as she is also known, wrote about her life over 150 years ago and her books are still popular today. In one of them she describes the kitchen in her large home. It was like a shed built at the back of the house and she writes that she was glad when it was replaced. The cook agreed — one day a mouse fell from the roof rafters into the soup (just one of many such incidents) — can you imagine!

## Sidebar

Inter

Needs overnight soaking

Serves 4–6

3 hrs 30 mins

Cook ♒

Hob ◎

Freeze ✳

## HAVE READY

- 225g (8oz) haricot beans (soaked)
- 2 litres (3½ pints) water
- 1 teacup of peeled, chopped tomatoes
- 1 medium sized beetroot – peeled, chopped
- 2 medium onions – peeled, chopped
- 1 parsnip – peeled, chopped
- 1 level teaspoon salt
- ¼ level teaspoon pepper

- large soup pot + lid
- liquidiser or hand blender
- chopping board
- sharp knife
- bowl
- colander or sieve
- wooden spoon
- teaspoon
- tablespoon
- saucer or spoon rest
- oven gloves

## TO MAKE

Put the beans into the bowl. Pour in enough fresh cold water to cover them. Place a plate over the bowl and leave overnight.

1 Prepare the vegetables (see pages 9 and 10).

2 Place the colander in the sink and pour the beans into the colander to drain off the soaking water. Rinse the beans under cold, running water and allow to drain.

3 Put the beans and prepared vegetables into the pan. Add 2 litres (3½ pints) of water. Put the pan on a medium heat and bring the soup to the boil.

4 Reduce the heat until the soup is simmering, cover with the lid and cook very slowly for 2 hours 30 minutes.

5 Stir every 30 minutes (use the oven gloves to lift the lid) and remember to hold the handle of the pan in one hand as you stir. Add more water if the soup is becoming very thick.

6  Use the oven gloves to lift the lid, add the salt, then liquidise or blend the soup until it is smooth (see page 13). Alternatively, mash well with a potato masher – hold it with the oven gloves as the steam may burn your hand.

7  Dip in a tablespoon and drop some of the soup on to a teaspoon. Wait until it has cooled before you taste it. Add more salt and pepper if you think it needs it.

8  When you are ready to serve your soup, bring it back to the boil and serve it hot in deep soup bowls or soup mugs with warm fresh rolls. Mmmmm!

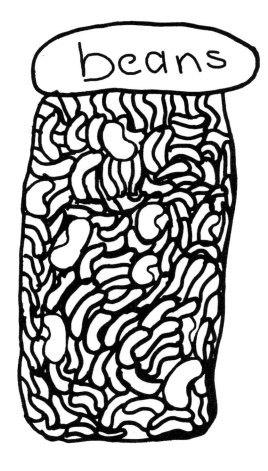

beans

# Neep Brose

'Brose' is a Gaelic word which means a porridge-like broth. 'Neep' is a Scottish word meaning a turnip or swede. The turnip was introduced into Scotland from Holland in the early eighteenth century and soon became popular because of its hardiness and frost resistance. This meant that at least one vegetable was available during the winter to add to the boring diet of different dishes of oatmeal.

Inter

Serves 6

1 hr 30 mins

Cook ≋

Hob ◎

Grill ⌘

E. Wok ◯

Freeze ✳

## HAVE READY

450g (1lb) turnips (swedes) – peeled, chopped

2 litres (3½ pints) water

50g (2oz) oatmeal

2 vegetable stock cubes

1 level teaspoon salt

pinch pepper

large soup pot + lid

baking tray

bowl

measuring jug

chopping board

sharp knife

potato masher

ladle

wooden spoon

tablespoon

teaspoon

oven gloves

## TO MAKE

1 Wash and chop the turnip (see page 10).

2 Put the chopped turnip and water into the pan. Place on a medium heat and bring to the boil.

3 Reduce the heat until the liquid is simmering. Cover with the lid and cook for 45 minutes until the turnip is tender – you can test it with a fork. Push a fork into the turnip and if it goes in easily, the turnip is cooked.

4 Turn on the grill to heat at medium. Spread the oatmeal on the baking tray.

5 Use the oven gloves to place the tray under the grill to toast the oatmeal. You will need to watch the oatmeal as it will cook very quickly, in less than a minute, and will burn very easily – stand ready with your oven gloves on!

6 Use the oven gloves to lift the tray from under the grill and set on a heat-resistant surface. Turn off the grill. Allow the oatmeal to cool for a few minutes.

7 Still using the oven gloves, carefully shake the oatmeal off the tray into the bowl.

8   Add the salt and a pinch of pepper to the pan and stir.

9   Pour a ladle of hot liquid from the pan over the oatmeal. Stir with the wooden spoon – it will form lumps called 'knots' or 'knotty tams'.

10  Mash the turnip with the potato masher, being careful not to splash yourself with the hot water.

11  Add the oatmeal mixture to the pan and stir well with the wooden spoon.

12  Dip a tablespoon into the pan and drop a little of the soup on to a teaspoon, wait until it has cooled, then taste it. Add more salt and pepper if you think it needs it.

13  When you are ready to serve the soup, bring it back to the boil and serve your Neep Brose piping hot. If you are feeling special, add a swirl of natural yoghurt to the soup! Pour a little into the centre of each bowl of soup and then quickly swirl it round with a fork – it looks good and tastes even better!

# Lentil Soup

The invention of the steam engine in the late eighteenth century revolutionised the life of a farm worker. After the stalks of grain had been harvested, a steam-driven threshing machine would travel round the farms separating the grain from the stalks. Neighbouring farmers would come to help and a big meal was provided by the host farmer. The food was made from the produce of the farm and so soup was always on the menu – usually lentil, tattie or broth.

Adv

Serves 6

2 hrs

Cook ♒

Hob ◎

E. Wok ○

E. Fry ❖

Freeze ✳

24

## HAVE READY

110g (4oz) lentils

2 potatoes – peeled, chopped

1 large onion – peeled, chopped

1 carrot – peeled, chopped

½ turnip – peeled, chopped

2 litres (3½ pints water)

1 tablespoon sunflower oil

2 level teaspoons salt

pepper

large soup pot + lid

hand blender or potato masher

measuring jug

chopping board

sharp knife

potato peeler

plate

wooden spoon

tablespoon

teaspoon

oven gloves

## TO MAKE

1 Prepare the vegetables (see pages 9 and 10).

2 Pour the sunflower oil into the pan and place on a medium heat to warm for 1 minute. Add the vegetables and lentils and cook for about 3 minutes, stirring to prevent them from sticking (this is called 'sweating' the vegetables).

3 Add the water, stir well and bring to the boil. If you see any froth or 'scum' on the top, use the tablespoon to carefully lift it off and on to the plate. Throw the scum away.

4 Add the salt and pepper. Reduce the heat until the soup is simmering and put on the lid.

5 Cook for 1 hour 30 minutes. Use the oven gloves to lift the lid every 15 to 20 minutes and stir with the wooden spoon. Add a little more water if the soup is becoming very thick.

6 Turn off the heat and allow the soup to cool a little. Place on a heat-resistant surface. If you like your soup 'rough', mash it with the potato masher. If you like a smooth soup without lumps, liquidise or blend it (see page 13) with a hand blender.

7  Dip a tablespoon into the soup and drop a little on to a teaspoon, wait for it to cool before you taste it. Add more salt and pepper if you think it needs it.

8  Serve steaming hot with fingers of warm, freshly made toast to dip in!

# Barley Broth

Broth is a filling 'meal-in-a-pot' soup. When it was cooked in a large pot over an open fire, enough soup was usually made to last for two days. The broth which was eaten the day after it was made was called 'Cock-crown Kail'. I have searched many books but cannot find out what this means – do you know? Broth without meat was called 'Lenten Kail', because wealthier families did without meat in their soup as a penance during the Lenten season leading up to Easter.

Inter

Serves 6

2 hrs 30 mins

Cook ≈

Hob ◎

E. Wok ◯

E. Fry ❖

Freeze ✳

26

## Have Ready

75g (3oz) pearl barley

1 small, white cabbage – washed, shredded

½ medium turnip – peeled, diced

3 medium carrots – peeled, diced

1 large onion – peeled, diced

2 leeks – diced

110g (4oz) garden peas

2 tablespoon chopped parsley

2 litres (3½ pints) water

2 tablespoons lentils (optional)

2 level teaspoons salt

¼ teaspoon pepper

large soup pot + lid

colander

measuring jug

chopping board

sharp knife

wooden spoon

tablespoon

teaspoon

saucer or spoon rest

oven gloves

## To Make

1  Prepare the vegetables (see pages 9 and 10). Put the barley, turnip, carrot, onion, leeks, lentils (if you have some), salt, pepper and water into the pot. Place on a medium heat and stir occasionally until the soup boils.

2  Reduce the heat until the soup is simmering and put on the lid. Cook very slowly for 1½ hours.

3  Use the oven gloves to lift the lid and add the cabbage and garden peas. Add more water if the soup is too thick. Stir the soup and bring it back to the boil. Cover and simmer for another 20 minutes.

4  Lift the lid with the oven gloves and add the chopped parsley.

5  Dip a tablespoon into the soup and drop some on to a teaspoon. Wait until the soup has cooled before you taste it. Add more salt and pepper if you think it needs it.

6  Serve in hot in bowls with big chunks of fresh bread. If you like soup and dumplings, why not try this recipe with the recipe for little Green Dumplings on page 30. These are cooked in the broth and taste delicious!

# Accompaniments for Soup

The thrifty Scottish housewife made many different additions to soup
to make it go further and fill the family.
Here are some ideas for you to try.

## Grated Cheese

Grate some hard, strong (half-fat) cheese into a serving bowl. Place this on the table with your soup. Each person takes some cheese, sprinkles it on top of their soup and stirs, allowing it to melt into the hot soup. This is especially good eaten in lentil soup, red pottage, tattie soup and tattie drottle.

## Oatcakes

Pop a plate of freshly made oatcakes on the table. Crumble some oatcakes into the hot soup and stir; the oatcake will make the soup thick, like porridge. It is very filling and very tasty!

# Croutons

No food was ever wasted. Stale bread was often made into croutons
and eaten in soup. Make these tasty snippets just before your soup
is ready to serve.

## HAVE READY

4 slices of stale bread

½ tablespoon olive oil

saucepan

baking tray

warm bowl

bread board

bread knife

wooden spoon

kitchen towel

## TO MAKE

1  Place two sheets of kitchen towel on the baking tray to line it. Place the tray beside the hob.

2  Using the bread knife, cut the bread into cubes, ½cm (¼ inch) square.

3  Pour the olive oil into the pan and place on a medium to high heat.

4  Add one cube of bread. If it sizzles, the oil is hot enough. Add the other cubes of bread and keep stirring until they turn golden brown.

5  Turn off the heat and carefully scrape the bread out of the pan on to the kitchen towel on the baking tray. This will drain off the extra fat.

6  Serve sprinkled on top of the hot soup, or put the croutons into the warm bowl and bring them to the table with the soup, so that people can help themselves.

# Cheesy Crusts

*If you have lots of stale bread you could also make these delicious crispy treats! Have fun fishing for the Cheesy Crusts floating on top of the soup!*

## HAVE READY

4 slices of stale bread

50g (2oz) hard, strong cheese (half-fat)

baking tray

grater

bread board

bread knife

dinner plate

fish slice

oven gloves

## TO MAKE

1 Turn on the grill to high. Toast the bread on one side.

2 Use the oven gloves to remove the tray from under the grill and set on a heat-resistant surface. Reduce the heat to medium.

3 Grate the cheese on to the dinner plate.

4 Use the fish slice to place the slices of bread on the bread board. Cut each slice into four pieces with the knife.

5 Use the fish slice to place the pieces on the baking tray, toasted side down, and sprinkle with the grated cheese.

6 Use the oven gloves to place the baking tray back under the grill. Wait for a minute as the cheese melts and bubbles.

7 Take the tray from under the grill using the oven gloves and place on a heat-resistant surface.

8 Ladle the hot soup into warm soup bowls and then use the fish slice to carefully float the Cheesy Crusts on top of the soup. Cheesy Crusts are really good with lentil soup or broth.

Simple

Serves 4

10 mins

Cook ≋

Grill ⌘

29

# Green Dumplings

*Traditionally, these small dumplings were made in the spring from the tender young green shoots of nettles, dandelion leaves, turnip tops, or green shoots of corn or hawthorn. Cooked in the soup, they absorb all the great flavours while they simmer.*

Inter

Makes 10–12 dumplings

25 mins

Cook 〰

Hob ◎

E. Wok ◯

E. Fry ❖

30

## HAVE READY

110g (4oz) flour

25g (1oz) shredded vegetarian suet

1 level teaspoon baking powder

½ teaspoon salt

1–2 tablespoons cold water

1 teacup of chopped young green shoots (use a mixture of parsley and young spring onions)

mixing bowl

sieve

palette knife

fork

dinner plate

draining spoon

teaspoon

oven gloves

## TO MAKE

1 Place the sieve over the bowl. Sieve the flour and baking powder into the bowl.

2 Add the suet and green shoots and mix well with the palette knife.

3 Add the water and mix to an elastic dough, adding more water if the mixture is too dry. The mixture will look quite green.

4 Use the palette knife to divide the dough into 10 or 12 pieces. Rub some flour on your hands, take a piece of dough, roll it into a ball and put it on the plate. Do this with all the pieces of dough.

5 About 15 to 20 minutes before your pot of soup is ready, use the oven gloves to lift the lid off the pan. Use the draining spoon to gently lower the dumplings into the hot soup. Put the lid back on the pan.

6 Leave the dumplings to cook for 7 minutes then take the lid off the pan (remember your oven gloves!). Use the draining spoon and fork to turn the dumplings over. Put the lid back on the pan and cook for another 8 minutes.

7 Serve the soup with the dumplings floating on top.

# Forcemeat Balls for Soup

'Forcemeat' is a corruption of the French word *farce* which means a savoury mixture used as a stuffing for meat or poultry. Like the name suggests, the mixture for these little dumplings can also be used as a stuffing – try it with tomatoes, potatoes or aubergines. Traditionally, the ingredients for Forcemeat Balls depended on what was available in the larder and garden. See how many different versions you can make!

## HAVE READY

25g (1oz) vegetarian suet

110g (4oz) breadcrumbs (wholemeal)

½ teaspoon grated lemon rind

½ level teaspoon salt

1 level teaspoon chopped parsley (fresh)

1 level teaspoon chopped thyme or fresh mint

1 small egg

pinch of nutmeg

plain flour

mixing bowl

wooden spoon

grater

teaspoon

draining spoon

dinner plate

small plate

small bowl

knife + fork

oven gloves

## TO MAKE

1 Put the suet, lemon rind, herbs, nutmeg, salt and breadcrumbs in the bowl. Mix together with the wooden spoon.

2 Break the egg into the small bowl and beat with the fork.

3 Add enough of the beaten egg to the bowl to form a stiff mixture when mixed with the wooden spoon.

4 Divide the mixture into 10 or 12 pieces with the knife. Rub flour on your hands and then take a piece, shape it into a round ball and put it on the dinner plate. Do this with all the pieces of dough.

5 About 15 to 20 minutes before your pot of soup is ready, use the oven gloves to take the lid off the pan. Gently lower the balls into the hot soup using the draining spoon. Put the lid back on the pan and simmer for 15 minutes.

6 Serve the hot soup and Forcemeat Balls in bowls accompanied by plenty fresh crusty bread for a tasty light lunch.

Inter

Serves 4

30 mins

Cook ﹏

Hob ◎

E. Wok ◔

E. Fry ❖

# Mealie Tatties

*Traditionally, the main course of a meal was a bowl of hot, thick soup and to make it more filling and nutritious a large floury tattie was served in the middle of the plate of soup.*

Inter

Serves 4

30 mins

Cook ≋

Hob ◎

No Freeze

32

## HAVE READY

4 medium sized floury potatoes (e.g. King Edward, Maris Piper) peeled + washed

1 teaspoon salt

boiling water

stew pan + lid

colander

sharp knife

draining spoon

teaspoon

oven gloves

## TO MAKE

1 Wash and peel the potatoes (see page 10) and put them in the pan. Add the salt and carefully pour in the boiling water to cover the potatoes.

2 Put the pan on a high heat and bring the water to the boil. Turn the heat down until the water is just boiling and place the lid on the pan. Do not put the lid on tightly – tilt it a little to the side to allow the steam to escape and stop the pan from boiling over.

3 Boil for 15 to 20 minutes until the potatoes are tender. Stick a knife into them to test they are ready (see page 10).

4 Put the colander into the sink. Turn on the cold tap so that the water runs slowly into the sink to disperse the steam.

5 Wearing oven gloves, lift the pan to the sink and carefully empty the potatoes into the colander to drain off the water.

6 Still wearing the oven gloves, lift the colander, shake the potatoes and empty them back into the pan.

7 Put the pan on a very low heat to dry the potatoes. While they are drying, serve your soup into deep bowls.

8 Use the draining spoon to lift a potato and place it in the middle of each bowl. The potato is like a hot island in the middle of a sea of tasty soup. Eat it while it is still hot – it will create a fire in your tummy on a cold day!

# Oatmeal

Oatmeal was the staple grain of the Highlands. The Highlanders had little need for actual money because most of their trade was done by exchanging goods – this is called 'bartering'. Oatmeal was traditionally used to pay for things like rent and taxes.

The wealth of the Scottish clans and their chiefs was in the cattle and sheep which they bred, and the clans were always plundering one another and stealing the livestock. One of the clan chiefs, called Barrisdale, was very powerful and clever. He levied a tax which was called 'blackmeal' because it was usually paid in oatmeal. This tax was imposed on noblemen and landowners in return for protection from the cattle thieves who were in Barrisdale's power and, as long as the money was paid, the cattle were safe. Those who did not pay had to mount their own armed guard as they were certain to be robbed.

So the Scots had their own version of the Mafia in the sixteenth and seventeenth centuries! Some people think that 'blackmeal' is where our word 'blackmail' comes from.

# Mealie Pudding

The Highland clan chiefs owned very large areas of land. This land was split into smaller parcels and leased to 'tacksmen' who kept some of the land for themselves and let the rest to smaller farmers or crofters. The tacksman was responsible to the clan chief for the rent, called 'mail', which was usually paid in oats for all the land under his lease.

Traditionally this pudding was tied inside a damp floured cloth called a 'cloot' and cooked completely covered in boiling water.

Inter

Serves 6–8

3 hrs

Cook ♒

Hob ◎

Oven ☐ 15 mins

Gas 4, 350°F or 180°C

middle shelf

Freeze ❄

34

## Have Ready

225g (8oz) oatmeal

50g (2oz) vegetarian suet

1 medium onion – peeled, chopped

1 egg (or half a cup of water or vegetable stock)

2 level teaspoons salt

½ level teaspoon black pepper

pudding basin (medium sized)

large pan + lid

baking tray

aluminium foil

string

mixing bowl

chopping board

sharp knife

wooden spoon

teaspoon

teacup

oven gloves

## To Make

1  Arrange the shelves in the oven so the baking tray can sit on the middle shelf. Heat the oven to Gas 4, 350°F or 180°C.

2  Spread the oatmeal on the baking tray.

3  Use the oven gloves to place the tray in the oven to cook for about 15 minutes. The oatmeal will burn very easily – be ready with your oven gloves on to take it out quickly! Set the tray on a heat-resistant surface.

4  Pour 2 pints of water into the pan and place on a medium heat.

5  Put the oatmeal, salt, pepper, suet and chopped onion into the bowl and mix together with the wooden spoon.

6  Break the egg into the teacup and add to the bowl. If you do not want to add egg, half a cup of cold water or stock will do instead.

7  Mix it all together and then put the mixture into the pudding basin. Cover with aluminium foil (see page 12).

8  Make sure that the water in the pan is boiling then carefully (use oven gloves) lower the pudding basin into the pan. Turn down the heat until the water is just bubbling and put on the lid.

9  Cook for 2½ hours. Use the oven gloves to lift the lid every 30 minutes to make sure that the water has not boiled dry. Add more hot water if necessary.

10  Turn off the heat. Use oven gloves to remove the basin and place it on the chopping board.

11  Use the sharp knife to cut the foil covering off. Remember steam which could burn you will escape from under the foil so make sure you lift the foil from the side of the basin, away from your face.

12  Serve with Stoved Tatties and Bashed Neeps (you will find the recipes on pages 79 and 82).

# Oatmeal Cutlets

There was a law during the seventeenth and eighteenth centuries which entitled the landlord to a quantity of the crop of oats grown by his tenants in respect of that year's rent. The landlord or his bailiff would oversee the reaping of that grain to make sure that the full quota of good quality oats was handed over.

Adv

Makes 8 cutlets

1 hr

Cook ≋

Hob ◎

E. Fry ❖

## HAVE READY

110g (4oz) oatmeal

25g (1oz) flour

2 tablespoons chopped leek

teacup of milk (semi-skimmed)

level teaspoon salt

1/4 teaspoon pepper

1 egg

75g (3oz) breadcrumbs (wholemeal)

light olive oil or sunflower oil for frying

baking tray

frying pan

mixing bowl

palette knife

pastry brush

fish slice

3 dinner plates

teacup

fork

tablespoon

teaspoon

kitchen towel

oven gloves

## TO MAKE

1 Put the oatmeal, flour, leeks, salt and pepper into the mixing bowl. Add the milk and mix together to make a soft dough.

2 Leave the mixture for 10 minutes to allow the oatmeal to swell. The mixture will become stiff.

3 Divide the mixture into 8 equal pieces with the palette knife. Use your hands to shape each piece into a round flat cake and place on a dinner plate.

4 Break the egg into the cup, beat with the fork and pour on to a dinner plate. Next to this plate lay a square of kitchen towel and put the breadcrumbs on to it. Place a clean dinner plate beside the crumbs. Put the plate of cutlets beside the egg – now you have a production line!

5 Take each cutlet in turn. First put it in the egg and use the pastry brush to paint beaten egg over all the surface.

6 Carefully lift the cutlet from the egg into the breadcrumbs. Lifting the paper towel at the edges shake the crumbs round and over the cutlet making sure that it is all covered. Pat the crumbs on with the palm of your hand and lift the coated cutlet on to the clean dinner plate.

7 Repeat steps 5 and 6 with all the cutlets.

8 Pour 2 tablespoons of oil into the frying pan and place on a medium heat.

9 Cover the baking tray with 2 layers of kitchen towel and place this beside the cooker.

10 Test the temperature of the oil (see page 12). When it is hot enough use the fish slice to place the cutlets in the oil. Cook for 2 to 3 minutes until golden brown, then use the fish slice and fork to turn the cutlets and cook the other side.

11 Use the fish slice to lift the cutlets out of the frying pan on to the baking tray. The kitchen roll will drain off all the extra oil.

12 Serve your cutlets hot. Try them with baked potatoes and a Winter Salad (you'll find the recipe on page 114).

# Baked Oatmeal Omelette

*Before machines were invented to do the work for them, people had two methods of preparing oats to make oatmeal. One way was to separate the grain from the husks and toast it by the fire; this made a meal called 'graddaned meal'. The second method involved threshing the oats and drying the grain in a kiln. Graddaning was more wasteful but quicker and gave the oats a very distinctive toasted flavour.*

Inter

Needs soaking

Serves 2–3

1 hr 30 mins

Cook ⁓

Oven ☐ 1 hr

Gas 4, 350°F or 180°C

middle shelf

No Freeze

38

## HAVE READY

110g (4oz) breadcrumbs

3 eggs

1 medium onion – peeled, chopped

275mls (½ pint) milk (semi-skimmed)

25g (1oz) oatmeal

12g (½oz) butter

1 teaspoon chopped parsley

½ teaspoon chopped thyme

1 level teaspoon salt

¼ teaspoon pepper

1 litre (1¾ pint) pie dish

small pan

mixing bowl

small bowl

tablespoon

teaspoon

teacup

fork

oven gloves

## TO MAKE

1 Pour the milk into the pan and place on a high heat until the milk boils. Turn off the heat and place the pan on a heat-resistant surface.

2 Pour the hot milk into the mixing bowl. Add the breadcrumbs and oatmeal. Mix together and leave to soak for 1 hour.

3 Arrange the shelves in the oven so the pie dish can sit on the middle shelf. Heat the oven to Gas 4, 350°F or 180°C.

4 Break an egg into the teacup and pour into the small bowl. Do the same with the other 2 eggs and beat with the fork.

5 Add the beaten eggs and all the other ingredients to the milk mixture and beat well together with the fork.

6 Rub the butter round the inside of the pie dish and then pour the mixture into the dish.

7 Use the oven gloves to place the pie dish in the oven. Bake for 1 hour.

8 Use the oven gloves to remove the pie dish from the oven. Serve hot with crusty bread and butter. You could also serve this delicious omelette with a big dish of freshly grated carrots and a plate of Pickled Beetroot (see page 120).

# Oatmeal Fritters

*In feudal times, when tenants rented their land from their chief or laird, the laird's income from his lands was measured in 'chalders' of 'victuals' (food). Therefore, instead of using pounds and pence, the yearly value of an estate was spoken of as being worth so many 'chalders'. The annual rent of a farm was paid mostly in 'victuals' like oatmeal, butter and barley.*

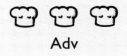

Adv

Serves 3

15 mins

Cook ≋

Hob ◎

E. Fry ❖

## HAVE READY

2 tablespoons medium oatmeal

1 tablespoon olive or sunflower oil

1 tablespoon flour

1 level teaspoon baking powder

1 level teaspoon salt

milk (semi-skimmed) to mix

frying pan

fish slice

baking tray

mixing bowl

wooden spoon

tablespoon

teaspoon

fork

kitchen towel

oven gloves

## TO MAKE

1  Put the flour, oatmeal, salt and baking powder in the bowl and mix with the wooden spoon.

2  Pour in the milk while stirring to make a creamy mixture which is like the thickness of double cream.

3  Pour the oil into the frying pan and set on a medium heat.

4  Cover the baking tray with a layer of kitchen towel and put this beside the cooker.

5  Test the heat of the oil (see page 12). When it's hot enough, gently drop tablespoons of the batter into the hot oil. Stand back from the frying pan as you do this – the hot oil may splash and burn you.

6  Cook for 2 minutes until crisp, then carefully use the fish slice and fork to turn the fritters and cook the other side.

7  Cook the fritters for another 2 minutes until they are crisp, then, using the fish slice, lift them out of the pan and on to the kitchen towel to drain.

8  Enjoy these fritters hot, sprinkled with grated (low-fat) cheddar or edam cheese to melt on top and lots of carrot fingers to dip into the cheese. Using stringy cheese like Edam makes this a lot of fun!

# Oatmeal Sausages

*Imagine if soldiers descended on your home because you couldn't pay the rent! After the harvest, landowners decided on the amount of crops they would charge as rent. This was called the 'feers-price'. If the tenant had not grown enough, he could pay the rest in money. However, if he could not pay it all, the civil magistrate would order a troop of soldiers to stay with him until the debt was paid (the number of soldiers depended on the size of the debt). It didn't matter how long the soldiers stayed, or how much of the tenant's food they ate, the debt still had to be paid in full! This punishment was first carried out in the reign of King Charles I (1600–1649).*

<table>
<tr><td>

Adv

Makes 4 sausages

I hr

Cook ∭

Hob ◎

Freeze ✳
(before deep-frying)

</td></tr>
</table>

## HAVE READY

110g (4oz) medium oatmeal

1 tablespoon sunflower oil

medium onion – peeled, chopped

1 egg

75g (3oz) wholemeal breadcrumbs

275mls (½ pint) water

1 level teaspoon salt

¼ teaspoon pepper

sunflower oil for frying

deep-fat pan or deep-fat fryer

saucepan

baking tray

3 dinner plates

sharp knife

chopping board

pastry brush

measuring jug

mixing bowl

teacup

fork

wooden spoon

draining spoon

tablespoon

teaspoon

kitchen towel

## TO MAKE

1 Chop the onions (see page 9). Pour one tablespoon of sunflower oil into the saucepan and place on a medium heat.

2 Add the chopped onions to the pan and cook, stirring all the time, until they are golden brown. Hold the handle of the pan in one hand as you stir with the wooden spoon.

3 Add the oatmeal and keep stirring until all the oil is absorbed.

4 Add the salt, pepper and water. Stir well. Reduce the heat to low and cook for 3 minutes.

5 Turn off the heat and use the wooden spoon to scrape the mixture out of the saucepan on to a plate to cool.

6 Break the egg into the cup and beat with the fork. Pour on to a dinner plate.

7 Divide the cooled oatmeal and onion mixture into four with the knife. Roll each piece into a sausage shape with your hands and put back on the plate.

8 Take two pieces of kitchen towel and put one on top of the other. Pour the breadcrumbs on top.

9 Now make a production line! Place your plates in a row – first the plate of sausages, then the egg, then the kitchen towel and lastly the clean plate.

10 Take a sausage and set it in the beaten egg. Use the pastry brush to brush egg all over the sausage.

11 Lift the sausage into the breadcrumbs. Lift the edges of the kitchen towel and shake the crumbs over the sausage. Gently pat them on with the palm of your hand.

12 Lay the finished sausage on the clean plate ready to be cooked.

13 Repeat steps 10, 11 and 12 with the other sausages, then put the plate of sausages beside the cooker.

14 Put 4 sheets of kitchen towel on a baking tray and place it beside the cooker.

15 Fill the deep-fat pan with sunflower oil up to the oil mark and place on a medium heat or switch on the deep-fat fryer to the correct temperature for sausages.

16 Test the temperature of the oil (see page 12). When the oil is ready, gently lower the sausages into the oil using a frying basket or the draining spoon. Stand back so the hot oil does not splash and burn you.

17 Cook for 3 to 4 minutes, using the draining spoon to turn the sausages. When they are golden brown and crisp, lift them out on to the baking tray to drain.

18 Serve your Oatmeal Sausages hot – any way you like. What about putting them in a finger roll with a wonderful salad mixture of grated carrots, apples and raisins and a few sweet cherry tomatoes – this is called a 'oatie dog' – Woof! Woof! Woof! Woof! Yowl!

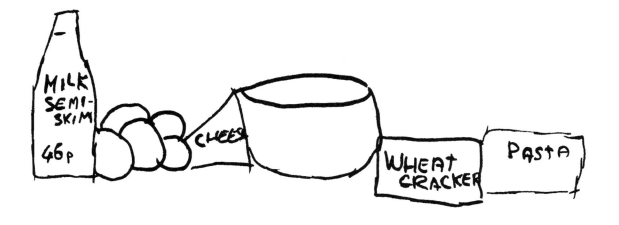

# Vegetarian Haggis

Traditionally, after a Highland wedding, the young groom would go round his friends and relations to beg for the things he needed to set up in his own croft – a cow, seeds to sow on the land, and so on. This was called 'thigging'. Included was, no doubt, a large sack of oatmeal and a quantity of vegetables to feed himself and his new wife until their croft could supply their needs.

When there was no meat available, the eighteenth-century housewife would make a savoury haggis-like pudding using oatmeal and any other vegetables she had.

Inter

Needs overnight soaking

Serves 3

3 hrs 30 mins

Cook ∭

Hob ◉

Freeze ✳

42

## HAVE READY

110g (4oz) medium oatmeal

50g (2oz) vegetarian suet

1 medium onion – peeled, finely chopped

1 medium carrot – peeled, finely chopped

12g (½oz) red lentils – soaked

1 level teaspoon salt

½ level teaspoon black pepper

25g (1oz) chopped mixed nuts (optional)

12g (½oz) wheatgerm

4 tablespoons warm water

large pan + lid

pudding basin (medium sized)

thick rubber band

chopping board

sharp knife

mixing bowl

small bowl

plate

sieve

tablespoon

teaspoon

aluminium foil

oven gloves

## TO MAKE

*Put the lentils into the small bowl. Pour in enough fresh cold water to cover them. Set a plate over the bowl and leave overnight.*

1  Prepare the vegetables (see pages 9 and 10). Put 7cm (3 inches) of water into the pan and put on a medium heat.

2  Hold the sieve over the sink and pour the soaked lentils into the sieve to drain off the water. Rinse with fresh cold running water and put the lentils into the mixing bowl.

3  Add all the other ingredients and stir well together with the wooden spoon.

4  Scrape the mixture into the pudding basin and use the back of the spoon to smooth the top.

5  Cover the basin with the aluminium foil (see page 12).

6  When the water in the pan is boiling, put on your oven gloves and gently lower the bowl into the pan. Reduce the heat so that the water is just bubbling and then put the lid on the pan.

7  Boil for 3 hours. Check every hour to make sure that the water has not boiled dry. (Remember to use your oven gloves to open the lid and keep your face away from the steam which will escape from the pan.) Add more water if you think it is necessary.

8  Turn off the heat. Use the oven gloves to remove the basin from the pan. The water will still be very hot so be careful.

9  Place the basin on a heat-resistant surface and, still using the oven gloves, carefully remove the rubber band. Lift off the aluminium foil from one side (not the front) so that the steam can escape away from you. Make sure you keep your face well back.

10  Serve the haggis while it is hot. Eat your haggis the traditional way with Stoved Tatties and Bashed Neeps (you will find the recipes on pages 79 and 82).

# Oatmeal Muffins

Oats were eaten a lot in Scotland – for breakfast, lunch and dinner! It might seem a boring diet but oats are very healthy and as they were so cheap, lots of recipes were invented to make them more interesting. These Oatmeal Muffins are certainly one of the tastiest I have found! Try adding a teaspoon of cinnamon or mixed spice and a handful of sultanas to the mix to make a spiced fruit muffin. Experiment with different fruit like raisins and dried chopped apricots. Delicious every time!

Inter

Makes 10 muffins

1 hr

Cook ∼

Oven □
12–15 mins

Gas 7, 425°F
or 220°C

middle shelf

Freeze ✳

44

## HAVE READY

½ teacup medium oatmeal

1½ teacups plain flour

4 rounded teaspoons baking powder

2 level tablespoons caster sugar

1½ teacup milk (semi-skimmed)

1 egg

1 tablespoon sunflower oil

pinch of salt

muffin or patty tins or baking tray

paper muffin cases

2 mixing bowls

teacup

fork

wooden spoon

sieve

tablespoon

teaspoon

wire cooling rack

oven gloves

## TO MAKE

1 Arrange the shelves in the oven so the baking tray can sit on the middle shelf. Heat the oven to Gas 7, 425°F or 220°C.

2 Lay 10 paper muffin cases on the baking tray or in the patty or muffin tins (these help keep the muffins in shape).

3 Place the sieve over the mixing bowl, pour the flour into the sieve and sift it into the bowl. Remove the sieve.

4 Add the sugar, salt and baking powder.

5 Put the oatmeal into the other mixing bowl. Stir in half a cup of milk and the sunflower oil. Keep stirring with the wooden spoon until you have a smooth paste.

6 Add oatmeal mixture to the flour.

7 Add the egg, the rest of the milk and beat well together. Spoon 2 tablespoons of mixture into each muffin case.

8 Use the oven gloves to place the tray in the oven. Bake for 12 to 15 minutes until risen and golden.

9 Use the oven gloves to remove the tray from the oven and set on a heat-resistant surface. Use oven gloves to set your muffins on the wire rack to cool a little. Serve warm. These muffins are absolutely gorgeous! Try splitting one and filling it with crushed strawberries or mashed banana.

# Cheese

About 400 years ago the Highlanders lived in groups of houses which they called 'townships'; the surrounding land was used for farming. The duties of each worker in the township depended on their social position. The chief was the most important person, and his assistant was called a 'tacksman'. The tacksman let some of his land to tenants who were a step below him in social rank. At the bottom end of the scale were folk called 'cotters' or 'acremen', who worked for the tenants in return for a small piece of land. Everyone had to work for the tacksman. The tenants worked on his land, repairing buildings and walls; they also worked as teachers, smiths, and did all sorts of other jobs. They passed work on to the cottars and acremen. The lowest and poorest were the farm servants called 'scallags'. For four days every week they had to work for the people above them. They received very little pay — in addition to the small piece of land they worked, a year's pay was usually some food, a pair of shoes, £1, and enough grass for one cow and her calf. A cow was very valuable, producing milk to drink and to make butter and cheese. Few scallags ever tasted meat, so cheese was extremely important in their diet as one of the main sources of protein.

Protein is important in our food. We need protein to grow strong and stay fit and healthy. Our bodies use it like a building brick to make muscles, tissues and blood.

# Cheese Frizzles

The farmland belonging to each township was divided into two areas called the 'infield' and the 'outfield'. The infield was used to grow crops of oats, barley, vegetables and a little flax which was used to make linen cloth. There were no artificial fertilisers in those days so the farmers spread their animals' manure on the infield to keep it fertile. The outfield was where the cattle grazed, and special pens with turf walls were made to keep the cattle safe. When all the grass was eaten inside the pen, the cattle were moved to another enclosure, and the one they had left was ploughed and cropped.

Adv

Serves 4

15 mins

Cook ≈

Hob ◎

E. Fry ❖

## HAVE READY

110g (4oz) medium oatmeal

110g (4oz) hard, strong cheese (half-fat)

50g (2oz) flour

2 teaspoons baking powder

1 level teaspoon salt

pinch of pepper

cold water

sunflower oil

frying pan

baking tray

mixing bowl

wooden spoon

tablespoon

teaspoon

grater

dinner plate

fork

fish slice

kitchen towel

## TO MAKE

1  Grate the cheese on to the dinner plate.

2  Put the oatmeal, flour, cheese, salt and pepper into the mixing bowl and stir in enough cold water to make a thick batter just like double cream (see page 13).

3  Pour one tablespoon of sunflower oil into the frying pan and put it on a medium heat. Place a layer of kitchen towel on the baking tray and set it beside the cooker.

4  Stir the baking powder into the batter mixture.

5  Test the heat of the oil with a piece of bread: if it sizzles, the oil is hot enough (see page 12).

6  When the oil is hot, very carefully drop in tablespoons of the batter mixture. Be careful to stand back so that the hot oil does not splash and burn you.

7  Cook for 2 to 3 minutes until golden brown. Use the fish slice and fork to turn the Frizzles and cook the other side.

8  Lift the Cheese Frizzles on to the baking tray to drain. Repeat steps 6 and 7 until all the mixture is used.

9  Serve hot with cherry tomatoes, baked beans, or for a quick snack, pop one in a warm roll filled with crisp salad.

# Melted Cheese Toast

In the summer months of May, June and July the laird's cattle were driven by the herdsmen to hill pastures to be fattened before being sent south to the markets or 'trysts'. The herdsmen's families followed the cattle, living in huts called 'shielings' and while the men attended to the cattle, the women made butter and cheese to keep for food in the long winter ahead.

Simple

Serves 3

15 mins

Cook ♒

Hob ◎

## HAVE READY

110g (4oz) cheddar cheese (half-fat)

2 tablespoons cream (single or half-fat)

3 slices of toasted bread

¼ teaspoon salt

pinch of black pepper

saucepan

2 dinner plates

wooden spoon

tablespoon

teaspoon

grater

knife

oven gloves

## TO MAKE

1  Grate the cheese on to a dinner plate.

2  Put the cheese, cream, salt and pepper into the pan and set on the cooker. Turn the heat to medium.

3  Stir the cheese and cream together using the wooden spoon. Keep stirring until the cheese has melted and begins to bubble. Hold the handle of the pan in one hand as you stir.

4  Turn off the heat. Remove the pan from the heat and place on a heat-resistant surface.

5  Lay the toast on the plate and set it beside the pan. Divide the cheese mixture equally between the 3 slices. Spread over the toast with the knife and eat at once.

6  This quick snack is very good to eat with a spoonful of chutney (see pages 118 and 119) and topped with sliced tomato.

# Cheese Pudding

During the fifteenth and sixteenth centuries the farmland was not divided into fields as our farms are today; it was divided into strips. Each tenant had strips in different parts of the tilled land around the township. Ownership of these strips was changed from time to time, so that everyone had a fair share of the good and bad land. This strip system was called 'run-rig'.

This recipe was written by the cook in a Speyside Shooting Lodge about 100 years ago – she made it for the staff to eat, so that she could use up stale bread and hard cheese.

Simple

Serves 4

50 mins

Cook 〰

Oven □
40 mins

Gas 4, 350°F
or 180°C

middle shelf

48

## HAVE READY

8 slices of stale bread

225g (8oz) cheddar cheese (half-fat)

3 eggs

25g (1oz) butter – softened

275ml (½ pint) milk (semi-skimmed)

1 level teaspoon salt

pinch of pepper

1 litre (1¾ pint) pie dish

mixing bowl

baking tray

tea cup

bread board

bread knife

grater

dinner plate

knife + fork

oven gloves

## TO MAKE

1 Arrange the shelves in the oven so the pie dish can sit on the middle shelf. Heat the oven to Gas 4, 350°F or 180°C.

2 Lay the bread on the bread board and cut off the crusts with the bread knife. Spread one side of the bread thinly with the butter and then cut each slice into four triangles.

3 Rub a little butter round the inside of the pie dish. Arrange a layer of buttered bread – butter side up – in the foot of the dish.

4 Grate the cheese on to the dinner plate and sprinkle some over the bread in the pie dish.

5 Repeat until all the bread is used, ending with a layer of cheese.

6 Break an egg into the teacup to check it is fresh (see page 8) and pour it into the mixing bowl. Do the same with the other two eggs. Add the salt, pepper and milk, and beat with the fork.

7 Pour the egg mixture over the bread and cheese in the pie dish. Put the pie dish on the baking tray.

8 Use the oven gloves to put the baking tray and pie dish in the oven and bake for 40 minutes. The pudding is ready when it is risen, golden brown on top, and feels firm when pressed gently with the back of a tablespoon.

9 Use the oven gloves to remove the dish from the oven and place the dish on a heat-resistant surface.

10 Eat hot with a fresh green salad – I like the golden cheese crust on the top!

# Nun's Beads

Traditionally the cattle trade between Scotland and England was the main source of income for the Highlands and Islands. Although the farming folk made their living by breeding and selling cattle, they seldom, if ever, tasted meat. They used the money they earned from the sale of the cattle to buy oats, barley and cheese, which would last them during the winter months.

This recipe is modified from one written by Mrs Dalgairn in 1829. Nun's Beads are traditionally deep-fried. This healthier version, which is baked in the oven, is a big hit with my son and his friends!

## HAVE READY

1 small, 250g packet of shortcrust pastry

75g (3oz) cheddar cheese (half-fat)

1 large egg

50g (2oz) breadcrumbs (wholemeal)

½ teaspoon salt

large pinch of ground black pepper

sunflower oil

mixing bowl

baking tray

dinner plate

rolling pin

pastry brush

teacup

wooden spoon

teaspoon

grater

sharp knife

fork

kitchen towel

oven gloves

## TO MAKE

1 Arrange the shelves in the oven so the baking tray can sit on the middle shelf. Heat the oven to Gas 7, 425°F or 220°C.

2 Rub a little sunflower oil over the baking tray using a piece of kitchen towel.

3 Break the egg into the teacup and beat with the fork.

4 Grate the cheese into the mixing bowl. Add the breadcrumbs, salt and pepper and mix together using the wooden spoon. Pour in enough of the beaten egg to bind the mixture together into one soft lump.

5 Take a teaspoon of the mixture and roll it into a small ball in the palms of your hands. Place on the dinner plate. Repeat until all the mixture is used.

6 Shake a little flour on the work surface. Place the pastry on the flour and roll it out thinly with the rolling pin.

7 Place a ball of cheese on the pastry. Cut a square of pastry round the ball leaving 2.5cm (1 inch) around it.

8 Pour a little cold water into the teacup. Use the pastry brush to brush water on to the pastry around the ball of cheese.

9 Use your fingers to lift up the pastry round the ball so that the pastry covers the ball. Press the corners and edges of the pastry together to seal the little parcel.

10 Repeat steps 7, 8 and 9 with all the balls of cheese.

11 Place the parcels on the baking tray with the join underneath. Brush with the rest of the beaten egg.

12 Use the oven gloves to put the tray into the oven and bake for 15 minutes until golden brown.

13 Remove from the oven, using the oven gloves, and set on a heat-resistant surface.

14 Nun's Beads are traditionally eaten warm as a savoury snack; however, they make a good lunch served hot with baked beans or grated carrots – you choose!

# Macaroni and Cheese

Until the late eighteenth century, the Highlander's dress was a long thick woollen cloak called a 'plaid'. It was almost the colour of the heather so that the wearer would not be seen. The plaid served as a cloak by day and as a bed at night when the men were out tending the cattle, hunting or at war. They would sleep three men together, with layers of their cloaks below them and then more layers on top!

Inter

Serves 4

1 hr

Cook ⌇

Hob ◎

Oven □
20 mins

Gas 7, 425°F
or 220°C

middle shelf

52

## HAVE READY

1½ teacups of macaroni

1 litre (1¾ pints) boiling water

25g (1oz) butter

110g (4oz) hard, strong cheese (half-fat)

2 level teaspoons salt

1 full teacup milk (semi-skimmed)

75g (3oz) breadcrumbs (wholemeal)

large pan

1 litre (1¾ pint) pie dish

knife

baking tray

grater

bowl

colander

plate

teacup

wooden spoon

teaspoon

oven gloves

## TO MAKE

1 Pour the water into the pan and put on to a high heat to boil. Add the salt.

2 When the water is boiling carefully add the macaroni, using the oven gloves. Stir with the wooden spoon and cook for 15 minutes. (Check the cooking instructions on the packet.) Add more water if necessary during cooking so that the macaroni does not boil dry.

3 Arrange the shelves in the oven so the pie dish can sit on the middle shelf. Heat the oven to Gas 7, 425°F or 220°C.

4 While the macaroni is cooking, grate the cheese into a bowl, add the breadcrumbs and mix together.

5 Cut the butter into small cubes on the plate.

6 Place the colander in the sink. Using the oven gloves, remove the pan with the cooked macaroni from the heat. Carefully, keeping your face away from the steam, empty the cooked macaroni into the colander to drain. Turn off the heat.

7 Spoon a layer of cooked macaroni into the pie dish.

8  Scatter some pieces of butter over the layer of macaroni and cover with some of the grated cheese and breadcrumbs mixture.

9  Continue layering the ingredients so that the last layer is cheese and breadcrumbs.

10  Pour the milk over the macaroni mixture and place the pie dish on the baking tray. Use the oven gloves to carefully put the tray in the oven and bake for 20 minutes until browned on top.

11  Remove from the oven using the oven gloves and serve hot.

12  You can make Macaroni and Cheese in all sorts of different ways. Try adding sliced tomatoes or onions to the layers of macaroni in the dish before baking. Whatever way you choose, Macaroni and Cheese is good to eat alone or with freshly grated carrots, mixed with grated apple and chopped tomatoes. There are lots of tasty macaroni dishes just waiting to be discovered – be inventive!!!

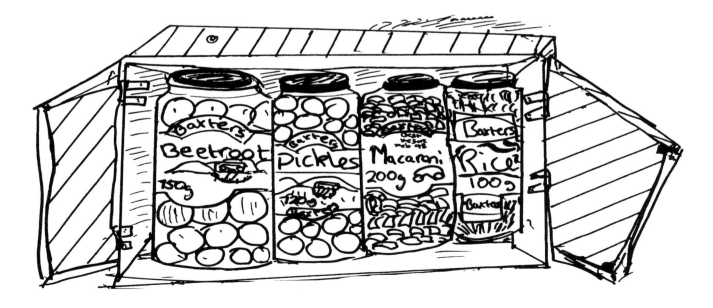

# Carrot and Cheese Toasts

*Cheese has always been a very important source of body-building nutrients. It contains a lot of protein which helps to grow muscles, flesh and skin, as well as calcium which we need to make strong bones.*

Simple

Serves 2

15 mins

Cook ∭

Hob ◎

No Freeze

## HAVE READY

50g (2oz) cheddar cheese (half-fat)

1 large carrot – peeled, grated

1 teaspoon margarine

¼ teaspoon ready-made mustard

2 slices of bread

salt + pepper

toaster

saucepan

3 dinner plates

wooden spoon

tablespoon

knife

oven gloves

## TO MAKE

1  Place the grater on one of the plates and grate the cheese on to the plate. Wash the grater.

2  Wash and peel the carrot and grate it on to the other plate.

3  Put the grated carrot into the saucepan with 2 tablespoons of water. Place the pan on a medium heat.

4  Bring to the boil and then reduce the heat until the carrot is just moving in the pan. Hold the handle of the pan with one hand and use the other to stir with the wooden spoon.

5  Simmer for 3 minutes and then add the grated cheese and mustard.

6  Season with a pinch of salt and pepper.

7  Stir all the time with the wooden spoon, holding the handle of the pan in one hand. When the cheese has melted and all the ingredients are mixed together, turn off the heat.

8  Toast the bread and place it on the clean dinner plate. Lift the pan off the cooker and set on a heat-resistant surface.

9  Divide the carrot and cheese mixture between the two slices of toast and serve. Eat while it is still hot and yummy. This makes a lovely snack on a cold day.

# Eggs

In 1730, Captain Burt was sent to the Highlands with his regiment and during his travels he wrote some very interesting letters describing his experiences. He often said that the inns and taverns were not very clean. In fact, in a hostelry in Edinburgh, he complained that the cook was 'too dirty to be described' and another person eating there said that 'if the cook were thrown at the wall, he would have stuck to it!'

Captain Burt also complained about the food served in the city inns, saying it was 'disgusting to see and smell'. He quickly found that fresh eggs were usually available and so he ate lots because they were cooked cleanly in their shells! The city streets were narrow with the houses built several storeys high. Each storey jutted out further than the one below it, which meant that the top storeys were almost touching allowing very little light through and making the streets very dingy indeed.

There was no sanitation or running water. Every evening at ten o'clock, a drum was sounded, giving the signal for householders to throw the dirt out of their windows into the street below. Anyone in the street was extremely lucky not to get soaked or worse. If you were in the street, it was customary to shout 'Hud your haunde!' in the hope that the people above would wait until you had passed. The smell was awful, although the streets were cleaned every morning, except Sunday – definitely a day to avoid a walk outside!

# Bread Omelette

Ordinary folk could not afford to buy many candles so they used fir twigs instead, burning them on stones round the fire. Fir twigs contain resin which burns slowly giving some light – hopefully it was enough to see to make an omelette to eat! Students used these twigs to do their studying and, so that they had enough light to read and write, they lit the twigs at both ends.

Adv

Serves 1

15 mins

Cook ≈

Hob ◎

56

## HAVE READY

| | |
|---|---|
| 1 slice of stale bread | frying pan |
| 1 large egg | small bowl |
| 1 teaspoon chopped parsley | tea cup |
| ¼ level teaspoon salt | fork |
| pinch of pepper | palette knife or fish slice |
| tablespoon milk (semi-skimmed) | tablespoon |
| 12g (½oz) butter | teaspoon |

## TO MAKE

1 Crumble the bread into the bowl. Break the egg into a cup, check it is fresh and add it to the bowl.

2 Add the milk, salt and pepper, and beat with the fork.

3 Put the butter in the frying pan and place the pan on a medium heat.

4 When the butter is melted and begins to bubble, carefully pour the mixture into the pan. Watch the mixture but do not stir it and slowly it will begin to set.

5 Loosen and lift all around the edge with the palette knife to check the bottom of the omelette. When it looks golden, carefully turn the omelette over using the palette knife or a fish slice. This is a little tricky so take your time. If you find this too difficult, use the palate knife or fish slice to loosen the omelette, then take a dinner plate, hold it face down on top of the pan and turn the pan upside down so that the omelette lands on the plate. Then carefully slip it back into the pan.

6 Cook for another 2 or 3 minutes to brown the other side.

7 Use the fish slice to slip it on to a warm plate – delicious! Serve it as a snack with juicy Baked Beetroot (see page 88).

# Sunshine Eggs

This is a recipe which has been adapted from the cookery book of Lady Clark of Tillypronie. The book was printed after her death and is a record of the recipes she collected between the years 1841 and 1897. Why not try collecting your own recipes – here's one to start you off.

## HAVE READY

I egg per person

6g (¼oz) butter

I tablespoon cream (single or half-fat)

I teaspoon breadcrumbs (wholemeal)

pinch of ground nutmeg

pinch of salt

ramekin dish

roasting tin

wire cooling rack

plate

I tablespoon

oven gloves

## TO MAKE

1  Arrange the shelves in the oven so the roasting tin can sit on the middle shelf. Heat the oven to Gas 4, 350°F or 180°C.

2  Carefully break the egg into the ramekin dish, try not to break the yolk.

3  Pour in the cream and sprinkle with salt, nutmeg and breadcrumbs.

4  Cut the butter into pieces on the plate and dot over the top of the mixture.

5  Place the dish into the roasting tin and pour in enough water to come halfway up the outside of the ramekin dish.

6  Place in the oven (using the oven gloves) to bake for 8 to 12 minutes to set the egg. (It should feel firm when touched with the back of a tablespoon.)

7  Use the oven gloves to very carefully remove the tin from the oven and place on the wire rack.

8  Use the oven gloves to lift the ramekin dish out of the water and serve with fingers of hot, freshly made toast. Eat your Sunshine Eggs for breakfast straight from the ramekin dish, dipping the hot fingers of toast into the delicious yolk. What a way to start the day!

Simple

Serves I

15 mins

Cook ∿

Oven □
8–10 mins

Gas 4, 350°F or 180°C

middle shelf

57

# Convent Eggs

*During the seventeenth and eighteenth centuries eggs were used as part of the bartering system to pay rent. As a result, property owners such as lairds, monasteries and convents often had a glut of eggs on their hands and it was left to the cooks to find ingenious ways of serving them.*

Inter

Serves 2

15 mins

Cook ≋

Hob ◎

Grill ⌘

## HAVE READY

2 hard-boiled eggs

275ml (½ pint) milk (semi-skimmed)

25g (1oz) butter or margarine

25g (1oz) flour

1 medium onion – peeled, sliced

½ level teaspoon salt

pinch of black pepper

50g (2oz) breadcrumbs (wholemeal)

1 litre (1¾ pint) pie dish

saucepan + lid

dinner plate + knife (or egg slicer)

plate

chopping board

sharp knife

wooden spoon

tablespoon

teaspoon

oven gloves

## TO MAKE

1  Peel and slice the onion (see page 9) on the chopping board with the sharp knife.

2  Put the butter in the pan. Place the pan on the hob and turn the heat to medium to melt the butter.

3  Add the onion and stir well until it begins to sizzle. Reduce the heat to low, put the lid on the pan and cook for 4 minutes.

4  Use the oven gloves to take the lid off the pan. Add the flour and stir with the wooden spoon.

5  Gradually add the milk, stirring all the time with the wooden spoon. Hold the handle of the pan in one hand and keep stirring until the mixture boils and thickens. Simmer and stir for 2 minutes.

6  Season with the salt and pepper.

7  Turn off the heat and place the pan on a heat-resistant surface. Turn on the grill at medium.

8  Slice the eggs with the egg slicer (or place the eggs on the plate and slice them with the knife). Lay the slices in the pie dish making sure each slice overlaps the other.

9　Pour the sauce over the eggs and sprinkle the breadcrumbs over the top.

10　Use the oven gloves to place the pie dish under the grill. Brown under the grill for 2 or 3 minutes until the top is golden and bubbling. Use the oven gloves to take the pie dish out from the grill and place on a heat-resistant surface.

11　Serve as a snack with hot toast and fresh juicy tomatoes.

# Egg in a Nest

The Scottish clans were like large extended families and all the members owed allegiance – which means loyalty – to the chief. When danger threatened, the chief would send a messenger round to his followers with a sign called the 'Fiery Cross'. The messenger passed it to the first clan member he met, and they would then pass it to the next and so on, just like a relay race. Each clan had a meeting place where they had to go as soon as they received the signal. They always took some food with them, including eggs which are easy to cook.

## HAVE READY

| | |
|---|---|
| 1 egg | baking tray |
| 1 slice of toast | small bowl |
| pinch of salt | teacup |
| butter for spreading | knife |
| | whisk |
| | fish slice |
| | tablespoon |
| | oven gloves |

## TO MAKE

1 Arrange the shelves in the oven so the baking tray can sit on the middle shelf. Heat the oven to Gas 4, 350°F or 180°C.

2 Separate the egg yolk and white (see page 8). Put the yolk into the cup and the white into the small bowl.

3 Add the salt to the egg white and whisk until you get a stiff mixture which forms peaks when dropped from the whisk – be careful not to overbeat the eggs.

4 Spread the butter on the toast. Pile the egg white on to the toast and make a hollow in the middle. Drop the yolk into the hollow.

5 Use the fish slice to carefully lay the toast on the baking tray and place the tray in the oven – use the oven gloves! Bake for 8–12 minutes until it has set and looks like a fluffy poached or fried egg. (The baking time depends on the size and freshness of the egg, so watch it carefully.)

6 Use the oven gloves to remove the tray from the oven. Set on a heat-resistant surface and pop the toast on to a plate, using the fish slice. Eat your Egg in a Nest while it is hot. Instead of toast, try dipping fingers of carrot and celery into the yolk.

# Cheesy Eggs

The moment the men of a clan received the signal of the 'Fiery Cross' (a sign that their clan chief needed them), they left whatever they were doing, collected their weapons, some food, and went immediately to their special meeting point. Each clan had a special 'war cry' which the bearer of the 'Fiery Cross' would shout as he went on his way. The MacDonalds shouted 'Freich!'; the Grants shouted 'Craig-elachie!' and the Mackenzies 'Tulliekard!'. When they were hungry perhaps they all shouted for Cheesy Eggs!

## HAVE READY

175g (6oz) breadcrumbs (wholemeal)

4 eggs

110g (4oz) cheddar cheese (half-fat)

1 level teaspoon salt

½ teaspoon black pepper

25g (1oz) butter

mixing bowl

1 litre (1¾ pint) pie dish

plate

teacup

grater

knife

fish slice

tablespoon

teaspoon

oven gloves

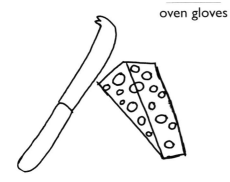

## TO MAKE

1 Arrange the shelves in the oven so the pie dish can sit on the middle shelf. Heat the oven to Gas 4, 350°F or 180°C.

2 Grate the cheese into the bowl and add the breadcrumbs, salt and pepper. Mix together with the wooden spoon.

3 Rub a little of the butter round the inside of the pie dish.

4 Spread the mixture evenly in the pie dish and make four hollows in the crumbs using the back of the tablespoon.

5 Break an egg into the teacup and then pour it into one of the hollows, trying not to burst the yolk. Repeat with the other 3 eggs.

6 Cut the butter into four pieces on the plate and put a piece on top of each egg.

7 Use the oven gloves to put the pie dish into the oven. Bake for 20 minutes until the eggs have set and the cheese has melted.

8 Remove the dish from the oven using the oven gloves and place on a heat-resistant surface.

9 Carefully lift the eggs out with a fish slice and serve each egg surrounded by the cheesy crumbs. Yum!

Simple

Serves 4

40 mins

Cook 〜

Oven □
20 mins

Gas 4, 350°F or 180°C

middle shelf

# Glendevon Savoury

*In the eighteenth century eggs were very valuable – both as a source of protein and as a way of paying for things like rent. With lots of eggs available, lots of different recipes were invented to use them up – perhaps this old recipe was one of them.*

🍞 🍞 🍞

Adv

Serves 8

35 mins

Cook 〰

Hob ◎

Oven □
20–25 mins

Gas 4, 350°F
or 180°C

middle shelf

62

## HAVE READY

| | |
|---|---|
| 8 eggs | 1 litre (1¾ pint) pie dish |
| 50g (2oz) butter (or margarine) | saucepan |
| 50g (2oz) flour | wooden spoon |
| 275ml (½ pint) milk (semi-skimmed) | tea cup |
| 50g (2oz) cheddar cheese (half-fat) | knife |
| 1 level teaspoon salt | grater |
| ¼ teaspoon black pepper | tablespoon |
| 2 tablespoons breadcrumbs (wholemeal) | teaspoon |
| | sharp knife |
| | chopping board |
| 5 fresh tomatoes | bowl scraper |
| 1 teaspoon sunflower oil | kitchen towel |
| | small bowl |
| | oven gloves |

## TO MAKE

1   Arrange the shelves in the oven so the pie dish can sit on the middle shelf. Heat the oven to Gas 4, 350°F or 180°C.

2   Rub a little sunflower oil over the inside of the pie dish using the kitchen towel.

3   Break an egg into the teacup, check it is fresh and pour it into the pie dish. (You will need to leave enough room for the other eggs to sit beside it.) Repeat with the other eggs, leaving a space between each one.

4   Place the butter or margarine in the saucepan. Place the pan on a medium heat to melt the butter or margarine.

5   Add the flour and stir in with the wooden spoon until the mixture is smooth.

6   Reduce the heat to low and gradually add the milk, stirring all the time. Hold the handle of the pan in one hand and keep stirring until the sauce boils and thickens.

7   Add the salt and pepper and turn off the heat. Place the pan on a heat-resistant surface.

8   Pour the sauce over the eggs in the pie dish.

9   Slice the tomatoes on the chopping board using the sharp knife (see page 10) and arrange over the top of the sauce.

10 Grate the cheese into the bowl, add the breadcrumbs and mix together. Sprinkle over the tomato slices.

11 Use the oven gloves to place the pie dish in the oven and bake for 20 to 25 minutes until hot and bubbling.

12 Use the oven gloves to remove the pie dish from the oven and place on a heat-resistant surface. This dish is traditionally eaten with oatcakes as a warm, filling and tasty snack. Try it yourself – or be as inventive as the eighteenth-century cooks and find something exciting to eat with your Glendevon Savoury!

# Tomato Eggs

Many of the townspeople in the seventeenth and eighteenth centuries kept
hens in their back yard. The hens and the eggs they laid were used instead
of money to trade for other goods – this is called 'bartering'.
This recipe has been adapted from the cookery book of Lady Clark of Tillypronie
written between 1841 and 1897.

## Have Ready

| | |
|---|---|
| 4 eggs | mixing bowl |
| 25g (1oz) butter | saucepan |
| 1 tablespoon milk (semi-skimmed) | 2 warmed plates |
| | teacup |
| 2 tablespoons tomato sauce (reduced sugar) | wooden spoon |
| 1 level teaspoon salt | knife |
| 2 large pinches of black pepper | fork |
| | oven gloves |

## To Make

1 Break an egg into the teacup (see page 8), check it is fresh and pour it into the bowl. Repeat with the other three eggs.

2 Add the milk, salt and pepper, and mix together with the fork.

3 Put the butter into the pan. Place the pan on a medium heat to melt the butter.

4 When the butter has melted, carefully pour the eggs into the pan. Stir with the wooden spoon until the eggs begin to set. Add the tomato sauce and keep stirring until the egg mixture is thick.

5 Do not allow the egg mixture to boil as the eggs will become rubbery, just allow them to cook until they are thick and creamy. Quickly and carefully remove the pan from the heat and place on a heat-resistant surface.

6 The egg mixture will continue to cook in the heat of the pan so quickly serve on to the warmed plates. This quick and tasty dish is lovely on hot toast or warmed split rolls.

# Potatoes

Potatoes were first brought to the British Isles by Sir Walter Raleigh from one of his voyages of discovery to South America at the end of the seventeenth century. The practice of growing potatoes for food was adopted in Ireland, from where the potato was introduced to Scotland and, by the middle of the eighteenth century, they had become an important and valuable food in the diet of the Scots.

# Harvest Pie

*The Highland men and women each had their own tasks to do. The men considered it beneath them to work in the harvest fields, and so the women did the reaping and other 'menial' tasks around the croft. This pie uses up a lot of left-over vegetables and was perhaps an easy dish to make after a hard day in the fields.*

Inter

Serves 4

1 hr 30 mins

Cook ∭

Hob ◎

Oven □
20–30 mins

Gas 5, 375°F
or 190°C

middle shelf

66

## HAVE READY

225g (8oz) potatoes – cooked, diced

1 onion – peeled, chopped

110g (4oz) cooked, diced carrots

110g (4oz) cooked cauliflower

110g (4oz) grated cheese

50g (2oz) breadcrumbs (wholemeal)

50g (2oz) butter or margarine

25g (1oz) flour

275ml (½ pint) milk (skimmed)

salt + pepper

1 litre (1¾ pint) pie dish

baking tray

saucepan

ladle

draining spoon

wooden spoon

teaspoon

knife

oven gloves

## TO MAKE

1 Prepare and cook the vegetables (see pages 9 and 10). Or, to save time, use frozen or tinned vegetables.

2 Arrange the shelves in the oven so the pie dish can sit on the middle shelf. Heat the oven to Gas 5, 375°F or 190°C.

3 Put 25g (1oz) of the butter or margarine into a saucepan and place it on a medium heat to melt.

4 Add the chopped onion and allow to cook for 2 minutes, stirring all the time with the wooden spoon. Remove the pan from the heat and set on a heat-resistant surface.

5 Use the draining spoon to put the onions into the pie dish and smooth over the bottom.

6 Spread the chopped carrots and potatoes on top of the onions and then add a layer of cooked cauliflower.

7 Put 25g (1oz) of the butter or margarine into the saucepan and put it back on the cooker on a medium heat to melt as you did before.

8 Turn the heat to low. Add the flour and stir with the wooden spoon until smooth.

9  Remove the pan from the heat and place on a heat-resistant surface. Gradually add the milk, stirring all the time.

10  Put the pan back on the heat and keep stirring until the sauce boils and thickens.

11  Add the grated cheese and keep stirring as the cheese melts. Add a level teaspoon of salt and a little black pepper.

12  Remove the pan from the heat and set on a heat-resistant surface.

13  Use the oven gloves to hold the pan handle then lift and pour the sauce over the vegetables in the pie dish scraping it out with the wooden spoon. Sprinkle the breadcrumbs over the top.

14  Use the oven gloves to set the pie dish on the baking tray. Carefully, lift the tray into the oven. Bake for 20 to 30 minutes until bubbling and golden on top.

15  Carefully remove the pie dish from the oven – remember to use your oven gloves! – and set on a heat-resistant surface. Serve your Harvest Pie while it is still hot. Harvest Pie is a 'one-dish meal' – serve it in warmed soup plates to keep it hot until the last yummy mouthful.

# Potato and Semolina Fillets

☰☰☰

Adv

Serves 4

1 hour

Cook ≋

Hob ◉

*Often, the women and children sang as they worked, doing their chores to the rhythm of the song. Keeping to the beat helped people to work together and it was frowned upon to fall out of time with your workmates. Sometimes the workers were accompanied by a piper – imagine rows of potato pickers singing to keep their spirits up and working in time to the skirl of the pipes.*

## HAVE READY

50g (2oz) semolina

4 medium potatoes – cooked, mashed

1 small onion – peeled, finely chopped

25g (1oz) butter

275ml (½ pint) milk (semi-skimmed)

1 egg

50g (2oz) breadcrumbs

½ teaspoon salt

four large pinches of pepper

flour

light olive oil for frying

saucepan

frying pan

baking tray

3 dinner plates

chopping board

sharp knife

wooden spoon

teaspoon

teacup

fork

pastry brush

palette knife

fish slice

kitchen roll

oven gloves

## TO MAKE

1 Prepare and cook the potatoes (see page 10) and chop the onions on the chopping board with the sharp knife.

2 Put the semolina and milk into the saucepan. Place on a medium heat and stir with the wooden spoon until the mixture comes to the boil.

3 Add the butter and onion and turn down the heat until the mixture is just bubbling. Cook for 10 minutes stirring occasionally and leaving the spoon in the pan (this will help to stop the mixture from boiling over).

4 Turn off the heat and place the pan on a heat-resistant surface. Allow to cool a little.

5 Add the salt, pepper and potatoes and stir well until you have a very stiff mixture.

6 Shake a little flour on to the work surface and scrape the mixture on to the flour. Shake more flour on top.

7 Divide the mixture into 8 roughly equal pieces using the palette knife. Rub some flour on your hands and roll each piece into an oval shapes about ½cm (¼ inch) thick. Put these on a dinner plate.

68

8  Clean the work surface.

9  Break the egg into the teacup, beat it with the fork and pour into one of the dinner plates.

10  Pour the breadcrumbs on to the kitchen towel.

11  Place the plates in a line – starting with the plate of oval fillets, next to it put the plate of egg, then the breadcrumbs and finally a clean dinner plate. You now have your production line!

12  Put a fillet into the egg and brush egg all over it. Use the fish slice to put the fillet into the breadcrumbs. Take the corners of the towel and shake the crumbs over the fillet, then pat them on with your hands. Lift the fillet on to the clean plate.

13  Repeat step 12 with all the shapes.

14  Wash the fish slice and place the plate of coated fillets beside the cooker.

15  Pour 1 tablespoon of olive oil into the frying pan and place on a medium heat.

16  Cover the baking tray with a sheet of kitchen towel and lay it beside the cooker.

17  Test the oil (see page 12) and when it is ready gently lift the fillets into the oil using the fish slice. Remember to keep your face back from the hot oil which could splash and burn you.

18  Cook the fillets for about 2 to 3 minutes until they are browned. Use the fish slice and fork to turn them and cook the other side.

19  Carefully lift each fillet out of the pan using the fish slice and place on the baking tray to drain.

20  Eat your fillets while they are hot with a crisp salad, crunchy carrot sticks, baked beans, spaghetti in tomato sauce – there are lots of possibilities! And next time you can make them into lots of different shapes – try using a pastry cutter. The sky's the limit!

# Tattie Scones

*In a time when most of the food eaten by the family was grown by the family, nothing was wasted. Leftovers from the meal were kept and made into another dish. A great favourite was to make Tattie Scones with leftover cooked potatoes.*

Inter

Serves 8

30 mins

Cook ≋

Hob ◎

Girdle ☿

No Freeze

## HAVE READY

225g (8oz) cooked potatoes, mashed

50g (2oz) plain flour

25g (1oz) margarine or butter

milk (semi-skimmed)

pinch of salt

sunflower oil for frying

frying pan or girdle

mixing bowl

wooden spoon

small pan

potato masher

rolling pin

wire cooling rack

fish slice

round scone cutter

dinner plate

2 tea towels

kitchen towel

oven gloves

## TO MAKE

1  Place the girdle or frying pan on a low to medium heat.

2  Put the margarine or butter into the small pan to melt – keep watching it as it will melt quite quickly.

3  Put the potatoes, flour and salt into the mixing bowl and add the melted fat. Mix well together using the potato masher. Add a little milk if the mixture is too dry.

4  Clean the work surface and dry with a clean tea towel. Shake some flour on to the surface and scrape the mixture out of the bowl on to the flour.

5  Shake some flour over the mixture then knead it together using your hands (see page 13) until you get a smooth ball.

6  Shake plenty of flour over the rolling pin and then roll out the scone mixture thinly – the thickness of a pencil. Shake on more flour if the mixture starts sticking to the rolling pin.

7  Cut into rounds using the scone cutter and use the fish slice to lift the rounds on to the dinner plate. Place the dinner plate beside the cooker.

8  Drop a little sunflower oil on to the surface of the girdle or frying pan and taking a thick piece of kitchen towel, carefully spread the oil over the surface.

70

9   Test the heat of the girdle or frying pan by sprinkling a little flour on to the surface. When the flour turns golden the temperature is correct – the girdle or frying pan is too hot if the flour burns and too cold if the flour remains white.

10  Use the fish slice to lay the scones on the girdle or frying pan and cook for about 3 minutes until golden. Use the fish slice to turn them and cook the other side for another 2 to 3 minutes.

11  Fold the clean tea towel and lay it on the cooling rack. Lift up the top half and use the fish slice to put the cooked scones inside the tea towel to keep warm while you cook the rest of the scones. Remember to oil the girdle or frying pan (step 8) after each batch.

12  Serve warm with home-made cheese and salad as a snack or try spreading them with home-made jam; Tattie Scones are also lovely with a hot bowl of soup. There are all sorts of things you could try – make the topping for Carrot and Cheese Toasts on page 54 and serve it on hot Tattie Scones instead of toast. You'll have fun testing different ideas!

# Potato Pasties

The Scots have always been extremely proud of their reputation as good hosts. Over the centuries they have traditionally gone to a great deal of trouble to give the best food and drink to their guests. There are stories of lairds who, not having much food themselves, went round all their tenants to collect enough food and drink so that they would have plenty to give to (and impress) their guests.

Inter

1 hr 30 mins

Makes 8 pasties

Cook ≈

Oven ☐

10 mins at Gas 7, 425°F or 220°C

30 mins at Gas 4, 350°F or 180°C

middle shelf

Freeze ❄

72

## HAVE READY

450g (1lb) potatoes – peeled, chopped

1 small carrot – peeled, chopped

1 small onion – peeled, chopped

1 stick of celery – chopped

350g (12oz) shortcrust pastry

1 egg

12g (½oz) butter

1 tablespoon chopped parsley

1 level teaspoon salt

¼ teaspoon pepper

mixing bowl

baking tray

rolling pin

chopping board

sharp knife

fish slice

knife + fork

teacup

saucer

pastry brush

teaspoon

oven gloves

## TO MAKE

1   Arrange the shelves in the oven so the baking tray can sit on the middle shelf. Heat the oven to Gas 7, 425°F or 220°C.

2   Prepare and chop the vegetables (see pages 9 and 10). Put all the prepared vegetables, parsley, salt and pepper into a bowl and mix together.

3   Shake a little flour over the work surface and rolling pin. Put the pastry on to the floured surface then roll with the rolling pin until it is the thickness of a thin china plate.

4   Lay the saucer on the pastry and cut round it with the sharp knife. Cut out as many rounds as you can. Knead (see page 13) all the scraps together and roll out again. Cut more rounds. Continue rolling, kneading and cutting until you have 8 rounds of pastry.

5   Divide the vegetable mixture evenly between the rounds.

6   Cut the butter into 8 pieces and place a piece on top of the vegetables on each round of pastry.

7   Pour a little cold water into the teacup. Dip the pastry brush into the water and brush round the outside of the pastry circles.

8  Fold the pastry over and seal the edges by pinching the pastry together with your thumb and forefinger.

9  Use the fish slice to lift each pasty on to the baking tray. Make a small hole in the top of each pasty using the point of the knife. This is to let the steam escape as the vegetables inside the pastry are cooking, and helps the pastry to become crisp.

10  Break the egg into the teacup, beat with the fork and use the pastry brush to brush each pasty with the egg. This is called a 'glaze' and will make the pastry golden and shiny when it is cooked.

11  Use the oven gloves to place the baking tray in the oven and bake for 10 minutes.

12  Turn down the oven heat to Gas 4, 350°F or 180°C and bake for another 30 minutes to cook the vegetables inside and turn the pasties golden and crisp.

13  Remove the tray from the oven using the oven gloves and set on a heat-resistant surface. These pasties are good to eat hot or cold. They'll make a nice change for your packed lunch or have them for a picnic! You can add any vegetable you like to the mixture inside the pasty. You can even try cubes of cheese, cooked rice, pasta, sweetcorn – almost anything! Invent your own pasty using your favourite vegetables!

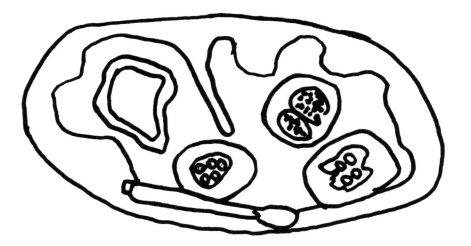

# Potato Casserole

Crofts were very important small farms. The people who lived on crofts produced the food they needed to survive. One of the most popular crops were potatoes: they kept well and provided food through the long winter. Cheese was another food which was made during the summer when milk was plentiful and kept for the cold months ahead. Put them together for this tasty traditional, simple meal.

**Inter**

**Serves 4**

**2 hrs**

**Cook** ≋

**Grill** ⌘

**Oven** □
**1 hr 30 mins**

**Gas 4, 350°F or 180°C**

**middle shelf**

## HAVE READY

| | |
|---|---|
| 675g (1½lb) potatoes | casserole dish + lid |
| 2 onions | potato peeler |
| 150ml (¼ pint) water | sharp knife |
| 150ml (¼ pint) milk (semi-skimmed) | chopping board |
| 50g (2oz) grated cheese (low-fat) | teaspoon |
| 1 tablespoon chopped parsley | oven gloves |
| 3 teaspoons salt | |
| black pepper | |

## TO MAKE

1  Arrange the shelves in the oven so the casserole dish can sit on the middle shelf. Heat the oven to Gas 4, 350°F or 180°C.

2  Peel and slice the potatoes and onions (see pages 9 and 10).

3  You are going to layer the potatoes and onions in the casserole dish. To do this you'll need to roughly divide the potatoes into four amounts. Divide the onions into three.

4  Spread a layer of potatoes on the bottom of the casserole dish and sprinkle a little salt and pepper over them. Spread a layer of onions on top. Repeat the layers of vegetables and seasoning, finishing with a layer of potatoes.

5  Mix the milk and water together and pour over the vegetables. Put the lid on the dish.

6  Use the oven gloves to put the dish in the oven. Bake for 1 hour 30 minutes until the potatoes and onions are soft.

7  Carefully, take the dish out of the oven using the oven gloves and set on a heat-resistant surface. Turn on the grill at high.

8  Use the oven gloves to remove the lid from the dish – be careful of the hot steam which will escape. Sprinkle the grated cheese over the top of the casserole.

9  Put your oven gloves back on and place the casserole under the grill for 2 minutes until the cheese is bubbling and golden.

10 Take the dish out from under the grill – remember to use oven gloves! – and serve while it is still bubbling. Add an oatcake, a glass of milk and some crunchy carrot and celery sticks to make a hearty supper.

# Cheesy Tatties

A hundred years ago shoes were very costly and so were not worn very often – even by the wealthier chiefs and their families. A story is told of a laird's wife who went barefoot to church on Sunday, while her maid walked behind carrying a pair of shoes and stockings. When she was in sight of the church, the lady sat down on a rock, put on her shoes and stockings and then went into church. After the service the lady returned to the rock and, after taking off her stockings and shoes and handing them once again to her maid, walked home barefoot!

Simple

Serves 2

45 mins

Cook ≋

Oven □
30 mins

Gas 6, 400°F
or 200°C

middle shelf

Freeze ✳

## HAVE READY

| | |
|---|---|
| 450g (1lb) cooked, mashed potatoes | 1 litre (1¾ pint) pie dish |
| 2 tablespoons milk (semi-skimmed) | mixing bowl |
| 75g (3oz) grated cheddar cheese (low-fat) | potato masher |
| | tablespoon |
| 25g (1oz) breadcrumbs (wholemeal) | teacup |
| | teaspoon |
| 1 egg (optional) | oven gloves |
| 12g (½oz) butter | |
| 1 teaspoon salt | |
| ¼ teaspoon pepper | |

## TO MAKE

1 Arrange the shelves in the oven so the pie dish can sit on the middle shelf. Heat the oven to Gas 6, 400°F or 200°C.

2 Put the mashed potatoes, milk, pepper, butter and cheese into the bowl and mash well together with the potato masher. (This is easier if the potatoes are still warm.) If you have an egg, break it into a cup, beat with a fork and add it too. It makes the potatoes really fluffy and light. If you don't have an egg, don't worry just add a little more milk.

3 Spoon the mixture into the pie dish and smooth it down with the back of the spoon. Sprinkle the breadcrumbs over the top.

4 Use your oven gloves to place the pie dish in the oven. Bake for 30 minutes.

5 Carefully lift the pie dish out of the oven using the oven gloves and place on a heat-resistant surface.

6 Serve hot. Cheesy Tatties make a tasty snack on a cold day; they are yummy too as a main meal with baked beans, oatcakes and a glass of cold milk.

# Vegetable Accompaniments

During the eighteenth century, a traveller in Scotland wrote that he saw a huge difference between the dwellings in the centre of larger towns and cities and the higglety pigglety assortment of long low cottages on the outskirts. These houses were built of rough stone with clay used as mortar, and turf covering the roof. They were badly constructed and inhabited by the poorest people who toiled long hours doing menial tasks for the more wealthy city dwellers.

Long hours and low wages meant that they could not afford the time or money to maintain their homes and, eventually, the cottages fell into disrepair and fell down. Undeterred, the now homeless occupants would build another similar dwelling beside the ruins and use the ground inside the ruin to make a sheltered vegetable garden or 'kail yard' as they were called. This vegetable plot was very important and probably one of their main sources of food.

# Buttered Barley

*During the sixteenth century, barley was prepared as a special dish to be eaten at Sunday dinner. It was made on a Saturday night when the barley was softened in water, placed in a hollow stone and the husks were beaten off with a wooden mallet.*

Simple

Serves 4

1 hr 10 mins

Cook

Hob

E. Wok

E. Fry

## HAVE READY

110g (4oz) pearl barley

1 level teaspoon salt

570ml (1 pint) water

12g (½oz) butter

stew pan

teaspoon

wooden spoon

## TO MAKE

1 Put the barley, water and salt into the stew pan.

2 Place the pan on the cooker, turn the heat to medium and bring to the boil. Reduce the heat until the water is just bubbling (simmering) and cook for 20 minutes or until the water has been absorbed and the barley is tender.

3 Add the butter, stir with the wooden spoon and simmer for another 2 minutes.

4 Turn off the heat.

5 Serve Buttered Barley hot with Potato and Semolina Fillets (see page 68) or Potato Pasties (see page 72). If you have any left, allow your Buttered Barley to cool and use it to make a great salad – mix it with chopped peppers, sweetcorn, chopped tomatoes, spring onions, garden peas, celery and any other vegetable you enjoy. Add some dried fruits like sultanas, juicy raisins or chopped apricots. Delicious!

# Stoved Tatties

During the eighteenth and nineteenth centuries shoes were a luxury only worn by the well-to-do and even they kept their 'shoes for Sundays only'! Folk went about barefoot and used their bare feet to help them to do their work. Women washed potatoes and other vegetables by the riverside with their feet, and farm workers put the hulls and beards of barley into a dry tub and ground off the stalks by twisting the soles of their feet backwards and forwards over them.

## HAVE READY

450g (1lb) potatoes (floury, dry varieties are best

e.g. Maris piper, King Edward, Pentland Squire)

12g (½oz) butter

1 level teaspoon salt

water

stew pan + tight-fitting lid

potato peeler

chopping board

sharp knife

skewer

draining spoon

tablespoon

teaspoon

oven gloves

## TO MAKE

1 Peel the potatoes with the peeler and place on the chopping board.

2 Use the sharp knife to cut them into equal sizes – about the size of a large plum.

3 Put the potatoes into the pan with 4 tablespoons of water and add the salt.

4 Cut the butter into small pieces and dot over the potatoes.

5 Put the pan on the cooker, turn on the heat to high and bring to the boil. Then turn down the heat to very low and put the lid on the pan.

6 Cook for 20 minutes and then test the potatoes with a skewer. The potatoes will be very soft all the way through.

7 Turn off the heat and carefully use the draining spoon to serve the potatoes. Eat hot with baked beans or oatcakes and put a fire inside your tummy on a cold day.

Simple

Serves 3

1 hr

Cook 〰

Hob ◎

E. Wok ◯

E. Fry ❖

# Stewed Onions

The Ochtertyre Housebook of Accounts written from 1737 to 1739 describes a Scottish kitchen garden which grew a huge variety of vegetables. A favourite dish of the day was to mix stewed onions with stoved or mashed tatties (the recipe is on page 79). Stewed Onions served with oatcakes are a traditional Scottish favourite – try some!

Inter

Serves 2

1 hr 20 mins

Cook ∿

Hob ◎

E. Wok ○

E. Fry ❖

## HAVE READY

2 large onions – peeled

570ml (1 pint) vegetable stock

12g (½oz) butter

12g (½oz) flour (wholemeal)

1 level teaspoon salt

pinch of pepper

stew pan + lid

small mixing bowl

chopping board

sharp knife

wooden spoon

draining spoon

teaspoon

serving dish

oven gloves

## TO MAKE

1 Peel the onions (see page 9), place them on the chopping board and cut them in half with the sharp knife. Put them into the stew pan and add the salt and pepper.

2 Pour in the stock and place the pan on a medium heat. Bring to the boil. Reduce the heat to low until the stock is just bubbling and moving in the pan, and put on the lid. Cook for 1 hour.

3 Mix the butter and flour together in the small bowl to make a paste. This is called a *beurre manié* and is used to thicken sauces and gravies.

4 Turn off the heat and, wearing oven gloves, carefully lift the stew pan on to a heat-resistant surface. Use the draining spoon to lift the onions on to the serving dish.

5 Remember to wear oven gloves to carefully place the pan back on the cooker and turn the heat to medium.

6 Stir the butter and flour paste into the juices in the pan. Keep stirring with the wooden spoon as the mixture heats and becomes thicker.

7 Dip in the wooden spoon and drop some of the mixture on to a teaspoon. Wait until it has cooled and then taste it. Add more salt and pepper if you think it needs it.

8 Put on oven gloves to take the pan off the heat and carefully pour the sauce over the onions in the dish.

9 Eat your stewed onions while they are hot and juicy. Next time why not serve them with tasty Cheesy Tatties (see page 76).

INGREDIENTS

1 egg
2 jugfuls of milk
teaspoon of honey
add 1 tablespoon of salt
mix well

Leave for 1 hour
Serves for 5

# Bashed Neeps

*One day a mill owner caught one of his employees stealing a turnip from a nearby field. He made the man eat the entire raw turnip there and then – the man never stole again!*

Inter

Serves 4

45 mins

Cook

Hob

E. Wok

E. Fry

## HAVE READY

1 medium sized turnip or swede

2 level teaspoons salt

boiling water

12g (½oz) butter

stew pan + lid

potato masher

chopping board

sharp knife

teaspoon

colander

oven gloves

## TO MAKE

1 Peel the turnip with the sharp knife (you will perhaps need some help with this as the skin can be very tough and thick), place on the chopping board and cut into pieces about 2cm (1 inch) square. Put the pieces into the stew pan with the salt.

2 Place the pan on the cooker and carefully pour in enough boiling water to cover the turnip. Turn on the heat to high and bring the water to the boil.

3 Turn down the heat so that the water is just bubbling and put the lid on the pan.

4 Simmer for 30 minutes until the turnip is tender (see page 10).

5 Wear oven gloves to carefully take the pan off the heat and place on a heat-resistant surface.

6 Put the colander in the sink and pour the contents of the pan into the colander to drain off the water. Be sure to keep your face away from the steam which could burn you. Running cold water into the sink helps stop the steam from blowing up.

7  Using the oven gloves, carefully tip the turnip out of the colander and back into the stew pan.

8  Add the butter. Then, holding the handle of the pan in one hand to keep it steady, use the potato masher to mash – or bash! – the butter and turnips together.

9  Serve hot. Bashed Turnips were traditionally eaten with Haggis (see page 42) or Mealie Pudding (see page 34). Why not try both to see which you prefer!

# Fried Parsley

*This recipe is hundreds of years old, but it is still made today by many of our top chefs! It can also be made using chopped kail instead of parsley.*

Adv

Serves 2

10 mins

Cook 〰

Deep-fat fryer

E. Wok ○

Hob ◎

## HAVE READY

50g (2oz) fresh parsley

sunflower oil for deep-fat frying

salt

deep-fat pan or deep-fat fryer

baking tray

dinner plate

colander

roll of kitchen towel

oven gloves

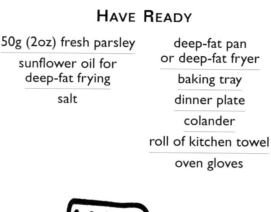

## TO MAKE

1 Wash the parsley, break it into large sprigs and use kitchen towel to dry it well.

2 Pour the oil into the deep-fat pan and place it on a medium to high heat. Place the frying basket on the dinner plate beside the cooker. Alternatively, put on the fryer to heat.

3 Put the parsley into the frying basket.

4 Cover the baking tray with a layer of kitchen towel and put it beside the cooker or fryer.

5 To test to see if the oil is hot enough, carefully drop in a piece of dry bread. When the oil begins to bubble and crisps the bread, the oil is ready. Do not allow the oil to get too hot – if you do, the parsley will burn.

6 Using the oven gloves, gently lower the basket into the oil and stand well back. When the bubbling dies down, the parsley is ready. This only takes about 1 minute.

7 Remove the basket from the oil, using the oven gloves, give it a gentle shake and tip the parsley on to the baking tray to drain. Switch off the heat.

8 Sprinkle with a little salt and serve at once with your favourite main course – good with anything.

# Curly Kail or Lang Kail

Kail (sometimes spelt 'kale') is a member of the cabbage family and its generic name is 'coalwort'. It is easy to grow and stands up to the Scottish weather so it has always been one of the main vegetables grown and eaten by the Scots, especially in the Highlands of Scotland. This recipe is best made with young and tender kail.

## HAVE READY

450g (1lb) fresh green kail

boiling water

1 level teaspoon salt

12g (½oz) butter

pinch of black pepper

stew pan + tight-fitting lid

colander

sharp knife

chopping board

wooden spoon

oven gloves

## TO MAKE

1 Wash the kail in cold running water. If you are using older kail, cut off the stalk. If the kail is young, the stalk is tender enough to eat.

2 Put the kail into the stew pan, add the salt.

3 Pour enough boiling water into the pan to just cover the kail. Place the pan on a high heat and bring to the boil. Reduce the heat until the water is just bubbling. Put on the lid and leave to simmer for 20 minutes.

4 Wash the chopping board and sharp knife.

5 Turn off the heat and place the colander in the sink. Wearing oven gloves carefully pour the contents of the pan into the colander to drain off the water. Leave to cool for 10 minutes.

6 Carefully tip the kail on to the chopping board. Chop the leaves roughly with the sharp knife.

7 Use the wooden spoon to scrape the kail back into the pan. Put the pan on a medium heat and add the butter. Stir with the wooden spoon. Sprinkle with a little black pepper.

8 Use the oven gloves to remove the pan from the heat and serve hot. Kail is very good for you – it contains lots of iron, calcium and other goodies which help you grow strong bones and fight diseases.

Inter

Serves 4 to 6

30 mins

Cook ⌇

Hob ◎

E. Wok ◐

E. Fry ❖

85

# Banffshire Potatoes

Long ago, girls who were employed as servants would be paid what were called 'board wages'. Their pay was not very much – 3 half crowns (which is only about 37 pence today), some oatmeal and potatoes to eat, and perhaps a pair of shoes to wear to church on Sunday – this was all they got for a whole year's work!

Inter

Serves 2

1 hr 30 mins

Cook ♒

Oven ☐
1 hr

Gas 6, 400°F
or 200°C

middle shelf

## HAVE READY

2 large potatoes

50g (2oz) breadcrumbs (wholemeal)

25g (1oz) softened butter or vegetarian margarine

2 tablespoons milk (semi-skimmed)

1 teaspoon chopped parsley

½ level teaspoon salt

pinch of pepper

pinch of mixed herbs

mixing bowl

baking tray

chopping board

sharp knife

wooden spoon

tablespoon

teaspoon or melon ball scoop

oven gloves

## TO MAKE

1  Arrange the shelves in the oven so the baking tray will sit on the middle shelf. Heat the oven to Gas 6, 400°F or 200°C.

2  Put the breadcrumbs, butter, mixed herbs, parsley, salt and pepper into the mixing bowl and beat well to make the filling.

3  Wash the potatoes well.

4  Cut a small slice off the bottom of the potato to make a flat surface. Then cut a larger slice from the top to make a lid.

5  Use the teaspoon or melon ball scoop to scoop out the inside of the potato to make it hollow. (Don't throw away the flesh from the inside of the potatoes – you can use it to make Potato Pasties, see page 72.)

6  Fill the hollow of the potatoes with the breadcrumb mixture and put on the lids.

7  Put the stuffed potatoes on the baking tray, standing them on their flattened bottom. Use the oven gloves to put the potatoes in the oven and bake them for 1 hour.

8  Use the oven gloves to take the tray from the oven and place on a heat-resistant surface. Remember to turn off the oven.

9  Serve hot – lift the lid and sprinkle some grated (low-fat) cheddar cheese on top to make a really delicious dish. Or, you can add the cheese to the filling if you like. I am sure you can think of lots of other tasty fillings – try adding sweetcorn, chopped spring onions, chopped peppers, chickpeas or baked beans.

# Baked Beetroot

We usually think of beetroot as pickled in vinegar and stored in a jar. Taste this recipe and you will see how juicy, tender and sweet freshly cooked beetroot can be.

Simple

Serves 4

1 hr 15 mins

Cook ≋

Oven ▢
1–2 hrs

Gas 4, 350°F
or 180°C

middle shelf

## HAVE READY

4 medium-sized fresh
young beetroot

baking tray
aluminium foil
blunt knife or spoon
colander
rubber gloves
oven gloves

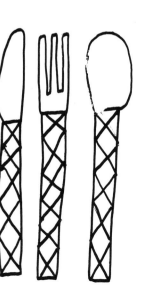

## TO MAKE

1  Arrange the shelves in the oven so the baking tray will sit on the middle shelf. Heat the oven to Gas 4, 350°F or 180°C.

2  Put on the rubber gloves (they will stop you from getting pink hands) and wash the beetroot well in cold running water. Take care not to puncture the skin of the beetroot. If you do, the pink beetroot juice will seep out – this is called 'bleeding'!

3  Wrap each beetroot in aluminium foil and lay on the baking tray.

4  Use the oven gloves to put the baking tray into the oven. Bake for 1 hour. Older or larger beetroot will take 2 hours.

5  Take the tray from the oven – use your oven gloves – and place on a heat-resistant surface. Allow the beetroot to cool for a few minutes then carefully open the parcels. Watch out for any steam!

6  Use the blunt knife or spoon to take off the beetroot skins.

7  Lift the beetroot into the colander using the draining spoon and run them under water to remove any pieces of skin. Use cold water if you like to eat the beetroot cold, and hot water if you would like to eat them hot.

8  Drain the beetroot well, then serve them with a crisp salad and boiled potatoes – the lovely fresh sweet taste of newly baked beetroot is one of my favourites!

# Puddings

By the eighteenth century, puddings had been introduced from France and it became the fashion to serve the pudding in a separate room after the main meal had been eaten. Before people ate puddings they simply had one meal made up of a large selection of main courses.

The working folk very rarely had such treats except on special days, like holidays, weddings, Christmas and New Year. When they did make puddings, they made sure that they made some lovely ones! There are some really yummy ones in this section for you to try – don't wait for a special day to make one!

# Apple Toast

When the daughter of a Scottish laird was going to be married, her father would give her a 'dowry' or 'tocker' – a sum of money or an expensive gift to give to her new husband. Sometimes the gift was given to the future husband's family so that they could judge whether or not their son should marry the girl – based on the size of her dowry! The girl would have no problem if her father was rich and she was the apple of his eye!

(see page 11)

## Simple

Serves 3

1 hr

Cook ≋

Hob ◎

Freeze ❊
(apple topping)

## HAVE READY

6 dessert apples (e.g. Gala, Braeburn or Cox)

25g (1oz) butter or vegetarian margarine

25g (1oz) castor sugar

2 tablespoons water

3 slices bread

soft butter or margarine to spread

baking tray

saucepan

wooden spoon

tablespoon

knife

fish slice

dinner plate

oven gloves

teaspoon

## TO MAKE

1  Peel, core and slice the apples (see page 11) and put them into the saucepan.

2  Add the butter, castor sugar and 2 tablespoons water.

3  Put the pan on a medium heat and bring to the boil. Reduce the heat until the apples are simmering and cook them for 5 minutes. Keep stirring while the apples are cooking. Turn off the heat.

4  Toast the bread in the toaster, or use the grill:

   a)  Turn on the grill to high and place the bread on the baking tray.

   b)  Use the oven gloves to place the tray under the grill to toast the bread. Watch it carefully to make sure it does not burn.

   c)  Take the tray out of the oven using the oven gloves and set on a heat-resistant surface. Turn the bread with the fish slice and place back under the grill using the oven gloves to toast the other side. Keep your oven gloves on and take the tray from under the grill and set on a heat-resistant surface.

   d)  Turn off the grill.

5 Lift the bread on to the plate with the fish slice and use the knife to spread with butter or margarine. Use the teaspoon to sprinkle the castor sugar over all 3 slices.

6 Take the plate of toast and place it beside the pan of apples on the cooker. Divide the apple mixture between the 3 slices of toast with the tablespoon, using the back of the spoon to spread the apples evenly over the toast.

7 Eat right away while it is still hot. Apple Toasts are good with thick, creamy (low-fat) natural yoghurt or fromage frais or try sprinkling with cinnamon for an exotic taste!

# Grosert Fool

Inter

2 hrs

needs to chill
for 1 hr

Serves 4

Cook ≋

Hob ◎

E. Wok ○

E. Fry ✦

'Grosert' is the old Scottish word for a gooseberry. It comes from the French word for gooseberry – *groseille*. 'Fool' is from the old Scottish word 'foull' derived from French *fouler* which means 'to press'. The fruit is cooked and pressed through a sieve to remove all the seeds and skin, and then it's mixed with cream or custard to make a smooth, thick, creamy dessert. This recipe uses gooseberries but you can make a 'Fool' with any fruit you like – try apples, rhubarb, strawberries or raspberries.

## HAVE READY

450g (1lb) gooseberries

110g (4oz) castor sugar

150ml (1/4 pint) fromage frais

150ml (1/4 pint) custard (low-fat, tinned)

mixing bowl

small bowl

large plate

wooden spoon

sieve

saucepan

whisk

bowl scraper

4 individual sweet dishes

oven gloves

## TO MAKE

1 Prepare the gooseberries (see page 11).

2 Put the gooseberries into the pan and place on a medium heat. When the fruit is simmering, turn the heat to low and cook for about 10 minutes until the fruit is tender. Turn off the heat.

3 Place the sieve over the mixing bowl and, wearing the oven gloves, lift the pan and carefully pour in the gooseberries – they will be very hot so pour them in slowly so that they do not splash and burn you.

4 Use the wooden spoon to rub the fruit through the sieve. You will be left with the seeds and skins in the sieve – throw these away. The fruit which has gone through the sieve into the bowl is called a 'puree'.

5 Add the sugar to the puree and stir well.

6 Cover the bowl with the large plate and leave to cool.

7 When the fruit is cool, pour the fromage frais into the small bowl and beat until it is smooth.

8  Pour the fromage frais and the custard into the fruit puree and 'fold' (see page 13) the mixture together. Stir very gently so that you still have stripes of custard, fromage frais and fruit puree.

9  Spoon the mixture into the sweet dishes and put into the fridge to chill for at least one hour before eating. This is a delicious creamy dessert — try popping the mixture into a plastic container to freeze into ice cream — wonderful!

# Cottage Potato Pudding

There is an old custom which took place on the evening before a wedding, called 'Feet Washing'. The bridesmaids came to the bride's home where they all washed her feet. They may have used potatoes left from the main meal to make something special to eat, and talked excitedly about what would happen the next day over a dish of delicious Cottage Potato Pudding.

Simple

Serves 3

1 hr

Cook ≋

Oven ☐
45 mins

Gas 4, 350°F
or 180°C

middle shelf

Freeze ❄

## HAVE READY

225g (8oz) cooked potatoes (warm)

50g (2oz) vegetable margarine (soft)

25g (1oz) syrup

25g (1oz) sultanas

1 large egg

1 litre (1¾ pint) pie dish

mixing bowl

wooden spoon

teacup

bowl scraper

oven gloves

## TO MAKE

1 Arrange the shelves in the oven so the pie dish can sit on the middle shelf. Heat the oven to Gas 4, 350°F or 180°C.

2 Put the potatoes into the mixing bowl and beat with the wooden spoon until smooth.

3 Add the margarine and beat well until it is all mixed in.

4 Break the egg into the teacup to check it is fresh (see page 8) and add it to the mixture in the bowl.

5 Pour in the syrup and beat well with the wooden spoon.

6 Stir in the sultanas.

7 Pour the mixture into the pie dish.

8 Use the oven gloves to place the dish in the oven and bake for 45 minutes.

9 Remove the dish from the oven using the oven gloves and place on a heat-resistant surface. Allow to cool a little and serve with (low-fat) custard, fromage frais or yoghurt. Now rest *your* feet and enjoy this real treat!

# Whim-Wham

Scottish lairds were not called by their surname but by the name of their house, estate or part of the estate. For example, if the laird's name was McKenzie and his estate was called Green field, he would be known as 'Greenfield'. This perhaps helped people to remember his name – 'Whim-Wham' is easy to remember and easy to make!

Simple

Serves 3

30 mins

No cook ☒

## HAVE READY

3 small individual sponge cakes

275ml (½ pint) thick fromage frais (low-fat)

25g (1oz) flaked almonds (optional)

25g (1oz) castor sugar

2 tablespoons apple juice

2 teaspoons grated lemon rind

3 orange slices to decorate

redcurrant jelly

2 mixing bowls

whisk

grater

plate

tablespoon

teaspoon

knife

3 glass dessert dishes

## TO MAKE

1 Cut the sponges in half and place in a bowl. Pour the apple juice over them and leave them to soak for 15 minutes.

2 Grate the rind from the lemon (see page 13) on to the plate.

3 Put the fromage frais into the other mixing bowl and carefully stir in the sugar and 2 teaspoons of the grated lemon rind.

4 Put a spoon of creamy mixture into the bottom of each dessert glass. You are going to layer the other ingredients on top. Cover the creamy mixture with a layer of soaked sponge, then add a layer of redcurrant jelly.

5 Add another layer of creamy mixture, sponge, redcurrant jelly and finish with a final layer of creamy mixture.

6 Place the glasses in the fridge to chill until you are ready to serve.

7 Just before you serve your Whim-Wham, sprinkle flaked almonds on top and decorate with a twisted slice of orange.

# Seafoam Pudding

In eighteenth century Scotland the working folk did not have fancy weddings – the ceremony was very simple indeed – the bride, groom and best man went to the church where the couple were married. They had no guests, no ring and no party but maybe they had a special pudding to celebrate! You can make this recipe with orange juice instead of lemon and a little grated lemon (or orange) rind will give a stronger flavour.

Inter

Serves 4

45 mins
and I hr to cool

Cook 〰

Hob ◎

E. Wok ◯

E. Fry ❖

96

## HAVE READY

570ml (1 pint) water
50g (2oz) cornflour
75g (3oz) sugar
juice of 1 lemon
2 egg whites

saucepan
teacup
teaspoon
wooden spoon
lemon squeezer
serving dish
2 mixing bowls
whisk
oven gloves

## TO MAKE

1  Put the cornflour into the teacup and mix it with a little of the water.

2  Pour the rest of the water into the pan, and add the sugar and lemon juice.

3  Set the pan on a medium heat and bring almost to boiling point – until the water starts to move and small bubbles appear.

4  Pour in the cornflour mixture stirring all the time with the wooden spoon (hold the pan handle in one hand as you stir). Reduce the heat and simmer for 2 minutes – keep stirring to stop lumps from forming as the mixture thickens.

5  Use the oven gloves to take the pan off the heat and set on a heat-resistant surface.

6  Still using the oven gloves, slowly and carefully pour the mixture into the bowl and leave to cool.

7  When the lemon mixture is cold, separate the egg whites from the yolk (see page 8). Set the yolks to one side and put the egg whites into the other bowl and whisk until stiff.

**8** Fold (see page 13) the whites gently into the cold lemon mixture and then pour into the serving dish.

**9** Chill in the fridge for 1 hour and then serve with creamy thick natural yoghurt (low-fat). (Don't throw away the egg yolks, try using them instead of the whole egg to make Nun's Beads on page 50.)

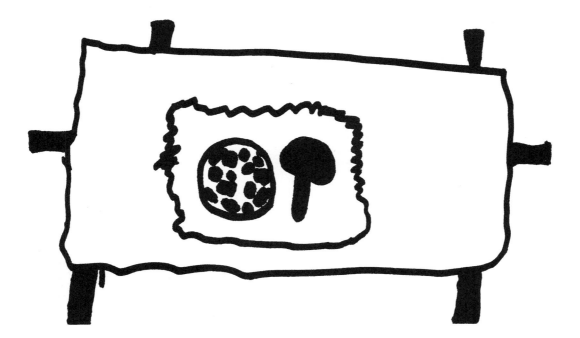

# Burnt Cream

Burnt Cream was first made in a country house in Aberdeenshire. Since then cooks have changed the original flavour by adding a cinnamon stick or orange zest. This recipe has also been adapted from the first written recipe.

Inter

Serves 3

1 hr

Cook ≋

Grill ⌘

Oven ☐
35–40 mins

Gas 4, 350°F
or 180°C

middle shelf

## HAVE READY

2 large or 3 medium sized eggs

150ml (¼ pint) milk (semi-skimmed)

150ml (¼ pint) single cream

25g (1oz) castor sugar

1 litre (1¾ pint) pie dish

roasting tin

saucepan

bowl

sieve

teacup

tea towel

knife + fork

oven gloves

## TO MAKE

1  Arrange the shelves in the oven so the pie dish can sit on the middle shelf. Heat the oven to Gas 4, 350°F or 180°C.

2  Break an egg into the teacup and pour into the bowl. Repeat with the other egg, then beat together with the fork.

3  Pour the milk and cream into the saucepan and place on a medium heat. Heat for a few minutes. The liquid should feel neither warm nor cold when you dip in your finger (this is called 'tepid' or at 'blood heat'). Turn off the heat, take the pan off the cooker and set on a heat-resistant surface.

4  Pour the liquid over the eggs in the bowl and beat together with the fork.

5  Pour everything through the sieve into the pie dish (this is called 'straining' and will remove any lumpy pieces of egg from the mixture).

6  Lift the pie dish into the roasting tin and pour in enough warm water to reach about one quarter of the way up the side of the dish. This is called a 'water bath'.

7  Carefully, using the oven gloves, place the tin in the oven. Bake for 35 to 45 minutes until the custard is set. (You can test it by sticking in the blade of a knife. If you take the knife out and the blade is clean, with no uncooked egg mixture on it, the custard has set.)

8  Set a doubled tea towel beside the cooker. Very carefully take the tin from the oven using the oven gloves and set on a heat-resistant surface.

9  Still using the oven gloves, lift the pie dish out of the water and set on the tea towel to dry the bottom.

10  Turn on the grill at high.

11  Sprinkle a thick layer of castor sugar over the top of the custard, put on your oven gloves and place the dish under the hot grill. The sugar will melt and turn brown. This does not take long – just a few minutes.

12  As soon as the sugar has turned brown take the pudding out from the grill, using the oven gloves. Remember to turn off the grill.

13  Allow to cool before eating as the hot sugar could burn your mouth. Eat warm – it is a lovely sensation to bite through the crispy sugar on top to find the lovely creamy custard underneath!

# Penny Saucer Pancakes

In the days when most large houses had servants, the Master and Mistress of the house would sometimes host the wedding of a favourite servant maid and hold what was called a 'Penny Wedding'. On the wedding day they would invite friends and relations to a meal followed by music and dancing in the evening. The bride kissed every man in the room and, at the end of the party, all the guests put money into a dish. The cost of the celebration was subtracted from the money and the remainder was given to the servant maid and her new husband as a gift with which to begin their married life. Pennies were a lot bigger then, but not as big as these pancakes!

Inter

45 mins

Makes 6 pancakes

Cook ∿

Oven □
20 mins

Gas 6, 400°F
or 200°C

middle shelf

Freeze ❊
(before spreading)

**100**

## Have Ready

25g (1oz) butter or vegetarian margarine (soft)

110g (4oz) plain flour

1 dessertspoon castor sugar

275ml (½ pint) milk (semi-skimmed)

2 eggs

sunflower oil

jar of jam (flavour of your choice)

mixing bowl

baking tray

wire cooling rack

wooden spoon

dessert spoon

6 saucers

teacup

sieve

pastry brush

oven gloves

## To Make

1 Arrange the shelves in the oven so the baking tray can sit on the middle shelf. Heat the oven to Gas 6, 400°F or 200°C.

2 Put the butter (or margarine) and sugar into the mixing bowl and beat well with the wooden spoon until the mixture becomes light and fluffy. This is called 'creaming' and will take a few minutes.

3 Break an egg into the teacup, pour it into the bowl with the sugar and margarine and beat with the wooden spoon.

4 Repeat with the second egg.

5 Place the sieve over the bowl, pour in the flour and sieve it into the bowl (see page 14). Remove the sieve and beat the mixture.

6 Stir in the milk to make a creamy batter.

7 Wash and dry the teacup, pour in a little oil and use the pastry brush to brush a little oil on to each saucer. Lay the saucers on the baking tray.

8   Use the ladle to pour the batter on to the saucers.

9   Use the oven gloves to place the tray in the oven. Bake for 20 minutes until golden brown.

10  Remove from the oven, using the oven gloves, and set on a heat-resistant surface. Allow to cool a little then, keeping your oven gloves on, lift a saucer from the tray, turn it upside down on to the wire cooling rack and let the pancake fall off. If it sticks, carefully ease round the edge with the blade of a knife and try again.

11  Spread the warm pancake with jam and fold it over. Repeat with the other pancakes.

12  There are lots of fillings you can try in your pancakes, here are a few to start you off – crushed strawberries, grated apple with cinnamon and sultanas, or mashed banana.

# Rhubarb and Tapioca

*The first rhubarb of the season was greatly prized – the thin, delicate pink stalks were washed, chopped and lightly stewed with sugar. It was called the 'Spring Conditioner' since a dish of tasty stewed rhubarb was said to spring clean the digestive system and purify the blood.*

Simple

Serves 4

1 hr 30 mins

Cook ≋

Oven ☐
1 hr

Gas 4, 350°F
or 180°C

middle shelf

Freeze ✳

## HAVE READY

| | |
|---|---|
| 450g (1lb) rhubarb | 1 litre (1¾ pint) pie dish |
| 2 level tablespoons tapioca | baking tray |
| 75g (3oz) sugar | chopping board |
| | sharp knife |
| | tablespoon |
| | tea towel |
| | 1 roll aluminium foil |
| | oven gloves |

## TO MAKE

1 Arrange the shelves in the oven so the pie dish can sit on the middle shelf. Heat the oven to Gas 4, 350°F or 180°C.

2 Wash the rhubarb under cold running water and dry with a clean tea towel.

3 Cut the rhubarb stalks into roughly 2cm (1 inch) pieces and put them into the pie dish. Put the pie dish on to the baking tray.

4 Sprinkle the sugar and tapioca over the rhubarb. Pour cold water into the pie dish until it is three quarters full and stir everything together. Cover the dish with aluminium foil, making sure to press the foil around the edge of the pie dish, and use the sharp knife to pierce a small hole in the foil to allow the steam to escape.

5 Use the oven gloves to place the tray (and dish) in the oven and bake for 1 hour until the rhubarb is tender and the tapioca has cooked to a jelly-like consistency.

6 Use the oven gloves to lift the tray from the oven and set on a heat-resistant surface. Very carefully open the foil – open it at the side of the dish, away from your face, so that the steam can escape and not burn you.

7 Serve hot with (low-fat) custard or ice cream, or leave it to cool, chill it in the fridge for a few hours and eat it cold.

# Bread, Butter and Jam Pudding

*On the signing of the Auld Alliance (23 October 1295) France and Scotland formed a close relationship. Some French words found their way into the Scottish language. For example, doors were also called 'ports' (from the French la porte), a field was called a 'park' (le parc), even today puddings can also be called 'desserts' (le dessert) – how many more do you know?*

## HAVE READY

6 slices of bread

25g (1oz) soft butter or vegetarian margarine

2 tablespoons of low-sugar, high-fruit jam (flavour of your choice)

25g (1oz) castor sugar

2 eggs

275ml (½ pint) milk (semi-skimmed)

1 litre (1¾ pint) pie dish

baking tray

teacup

knife + fork

bread board

measuring jug

oven gloves

## TO MAKE

1  Arrange the shelves in the oven so the pie dish can sit on the middle shelf. Heat the oven to Gas 5, 375°F or 190°C.

2  Spread the bread on one side with butter and then jam. Cut each slice into four fingers. Then cut across the fingers to make six squares. Put all the bread into the pie dish.

3  Sprinkle the sugar over the bread.

4  Break an egg into the cup and then pour it into the bowl. Do the same with the other egg and beat with the fork.

5  Measure the milk into the jug, add the beaten eggs and beat together with the fork.

6  Lift the pie dish on to the baking tray. Pour the egg mixture over the bread in the dish.

7  Use the oven gloves to place the pie dish and baking tray in the oven.

8  Bake for 30 minutes until risen and golden.

9  Use the oven gloves to take the pie dish out of the oven and place on a heat-resistant surface.

10 Leave to cool for a few minutes before serving as the jam is very hot and might burn your mouth. This pudding is good to eat alone or with some plump raisins scattered on top. Yum!

Inter

Serves 4

1 hr

Cook ≈

Oven ☐ 30 mins

Gas 5, 375°F or 190°C

middle shelf

**103**

# Apple Balls

Ever fancied a whole apple pie to yourself? Well here's an apple pie with a difference! Individual apples covered in pastry and filled with the filling of your choice. Choose what you want for your own apple ball – try mincemeat, raisins, chopped apricots, or sultanas – the choice is endless. Why not make a different one for each person!

Inter

Serves 3

1 hr

Cook ∿

Oven ▢
30 mins

Gas 5, 375°F
or 190°C

middle shelf

Freeze ❋

## HAVE READY

175g (6oz) shortcrust pastry

3 medium sized eating apples (Granny Smiths or Cox are best)

1 egg

your choice of filling

castor sugar to decorate

rolling pin

potato peeler or apple corer

sharp knife

chopping board

baking tray

fish slice

pastry brush

teacup

fork

2 tea towels

oven gloves

## TO MAKE

1 Arrange the shelves in the oven so the baking tray will sit on the middle shelf. Heat the oven to Gas 5, 375°F or 190°C.

2 Wash the skins of the apples well and dry them on a clean tea towel. Use the corer to remove the core or cut round it using the point of a potato peeler (push it further and further through the apple until you can push the core out).

3 Put your choice of filling into the hole left by the core.

4 Clean the work surface well and dry it with a clean tea towel.

5 Shake a little flour over the work surface and the rolling pin.

6 Divide the pastry into three equal pieces. Take one piece of pastry and roll it out into a circle large enough to cover the apple. Repeat with the other two pieces of pastry.

7 Place an apple in the centre of each round of pastry.

8 Pour some cold water into the cup and use the pastry brush to paint water over the pastry around the apple.

9   Now wrap the apple in the pastry – bring the edges of the pastry up to meet at the top and press the edges together in a join. Make sure all the apple is covered in pastry and squash the edges where the pastry overlaps to seal the ball. Roll the apple to make a neat shape. Do the same with the other apples.

10  Put the apples on the baking tray.

11  Empty the water out of the cup. Break the egg into the cup and beat it with the fork. Use the pastry brush to paint the pastry-covered apples with the beaten egg.

12  Use the oven gloves to put the tray into the oven. Bake for 30 minutes.

13  When the pastry looks golden, remove the tray from the oven using the oven gloves and place on a heat-resistant surface. Leave to cool for a few minutes.

14  Use the fish slice to lift the apples on to pudding plates. Shake a little caster sugar over the Apple Balls before you serve them – they are absolutely wonderful to eat hot or cold. See if you can you remember what you chose for your filling!

# Oatmeal Cream

The harvest labourers were often paid in kind. That is, they were given some of the grain (oats or barley) which they had just cut and made into sheaves. If they were paid in money, they got about two or three pence a day plus a meal which was usually made of oatmeal.
The flavour of Oatmeal Cream is very delicate. To give it a stronger flavour you can add a little grated orange rind and juice.

needs to soak for 30 mins

Serves 4

3 hrs

Cook ♒

Hob ◎

## HAVE READY

110g (4oz) oatmeal

275ml (½ pint) milk (semi-skimmed)

275ml (½ pint) creme fraiche (low-fat)

50g (2oz) sugar

1 heaped teaspoon gelozone (vegetarian alternative to gelatine)

2 mixing bowls

teacup

small saucepan

wooden spoon

tablespoon

teaspoon

bowl scraper

sieve

jelly mould or serving dish

oven gloves

## TO MAKE

1 Put the oatmeal into a bowl and cover with half the quantity of milk. Mix well and leave to soak for 30 minutes.

2 Pour the rest of the milk into a pan, sprinkle in the gelozone and mix well. Stir in 2 tablespoons of water.

3 Put the pan on a high heat and bring to the boil, stirring all the time. Hold the handle of the pan with one hand as you stir. Reduce the heat and simmer, still stirring, for 2 minutes. Turn off the heat, set the pan on a heat-resistant surface and leave to cool.

4 Pour the creme fraiche into the other bowl and beat with the wooden spoon until it is smooth.

5 Stir the oatmeal and milk. Place the sieve over the bowl of creme fraiche and pour in the milk and oatmeal mixture. Press it through the sieve with the back of the tablespoon until all that is left is dry oatmeal. Remove the sieve.

6 Add the sugar to the creme fraiche and oatmeal. Stir well.

7 Pour in the cooled gelozone, stirring all the time.

8 Pour the mixture into the serving dish or mould and leave to set in the fridge. Serve cold with fresh fruit like strawberries or raspberries, canned fruit, fruit sauce or stewed fruit – any kind of fruit at all!

# Christmas Recipes

'When Merry Yule-day comes, I trow,
You'll scantlins find a hungry mou;
Sma are our cares, our stamacks fou,
O'gusty gear!

'THE DAFT DAYS' BY R. FERGUSSON

Everyone eagerly looked forward to 'Christenmas' or 'Yule' as it used to be called. It meant at least half a day's holiday from work and the prospect of a specially prepared feast. Just as we enjoy traditional goodies at Christmas so did our ancestors hundreds of years ago. They would start the day with a hot bowl of Yule Brose (a thick, creamy porridge-like dish). Yule Bread was baked fresh before dawn on Christmas Day – it was like a flat crisp oatcake made in a round and cut into four pieces: the cutting line was meant to represent the cross. Lots of Yule Breads were made so that each member of the family got a piece – the superstition was that if you could keep the piece whole until the evening, good luck and good fortune would be yours in the New Year to come.

# Mincemeat

Mincemeat first appeared on our tables during the sixteenth century about the time of Mary Queen of Scots. Originally, mincemeat really did contain meat! – it was mixed with spices, fruit and suet. However, as time passed people's taste changed and the meat was replaced with citrus peel and fresh fruits like apples. Make your own mincemeat for Christmas – it tastes wonderful.

**Simple**

**Needs overnight soaking**

**Makes 5 x 225g (8oz) jars**

**30 mins**

**No cook** ☒

## HAVE READY

225g (8oz) grated fresh apple

225g (8oz) raisins

225g (8oz) light soft brown sugar

75g (3oz) sultanas

75g (3oz) currants

50g (2oz) mixed peel

50g (2oz) vegetarian suet

grated rind and juice of I orange

grated rind and juice of I lemon

6 tablespoons apple juice or brandy

I teaspoon mixed spice

I teaspoon ground cinnamon

¼ teaspoon nutmeg

5 x 225g (8oz) jars + screw-top lids

large bowl

large plate

sharp knife

chopping board

grater

lemon squeezer

wooden spoon

tablespoon

## TO MAKE

1 Wash and grate the apple (see pages 11 and 13) into the large bowl.

2 Grate the rind from the orange and lemon into the bowl (see page 13).

3 Place the lemon on the chopping board and cut it in half with the sharp knife. Use the lemon squeezer (manual or electric) to squeeze out all the juice. Throw away the skin and pips, and pour the juice into the mixing bowl.

4 Do the same with the orange.

5 Add all the other ingredients to the bowl and mix well with the wooden spoon.

6 Cover the bowl with the plate and leave overnight.

7 Stir the soaked mixture well.

8 Use the tablespoon to spoon the mixture into the jars. Screw on the lids and store for one week in a cool dry place to allow all the flavours to mingle before using.

# Home-made Mixed Spice

Dundee was a very important seaport from the fourteenth to the seventeenth centuries. Tall ships arrived in the busy port with exotic goods – fruits, spices, silks and many other unusual goods. Imagine the excitement as the ships docked and unloaded their wonderful cargo. Today you can easily buy the spices already ground, but at that time the whole spices had to be ground together with a rounded stone 'pestle' in a stone bowl called a 'mortar'.

Simple

10 mins

No cook ☒

## HAVE READY

25g (1oz) ground
black pepper

12g (½oz) ground
Jamaica Pepper
(sometimes called
Allspice)

12g (½oz) ground
ginger

12g (½oz) ground
cinnamon

12g (½oz) ground
nutmeg

12g (½oz) ground
cloves

jam jar + screw-top lid

bowl

tablespoon

## TO MAKE

1  Mix all the ingredients together in a bowl with the tablespoon.

2  Carefully spoon the mixture into a dry airtight container, like a jam jar, and store in a cool dry place ready to use. This mixture adds an exotic taste to mincemeat (you'll find the recipe on page 108), fruit pies (especially apple pies), fruit cakes, gingerbreads and biscuits. It's quick, easy and delicious!

# Mincemeat Pies

There is an old legend which says that if you eat twelve mincemeat pies between Christmas Day and Twelfth Night, the New Year will bring you good fortune! Make your own pies and eat your way to Twelfth Night!

Inter

Makes 14 pies

1 hr

Cook ≋

Oven □
15–25 mins

Gas 7, 425°F
or 220°C

middle shelf

## HAVE READY

225g (8oz) shortcrust pastry

225g (8oz) mincemeat

plain flour

1 small egg

pastry cutter – 5cm (2 inches) diameter

pastry cutter – 7cm (3 inches) diameter

baking tray

pastry brush

rolling pin

teaspoon

cup

knife + fork

fish slice

wire cooling rack

oven gloves

## To Make

1 Arrange the shelves in the oven so the baking tray will sit on the middle shelf. Heat the oven to Gas 7, 425°F or 220°C.

2 Clean and dry the worktop and shake a little flour over it. Place the pastry on the flour, shake a little more flour on the pastry and also on the rolling pin. Using the rolling pin, roll the pastry evenly until it is the thickness of a china plate.

3 Cut out 7 rounds of pastry with the large cutter and 7 rounds with the small cutter. If you cannot cut enough rounds, cut out as many as you can and then scrunch the scraps together and roll out the pastry again. Keep scrunching, rolling and cutting until you have enough rounds.

4 Put the smaller rounds on the baking tray and brush with a little cold water.

5 Drop a teaspoon of mincemeat into the centre of each round.

6 Cover with the larger rounds of pastry. Use your thumb and pointing finger to pinch the two rounds of pastry together – pinch all round the edges to make sure they are tightly sealed.

7   Break the egg into the teacup and beat with the fork. Brush the top of the pies with the beaten egg (this is called an 'egg wash') to make the pies all golden when they are baked.

8   Use the point of the knife to make two small slits on the top of the pies to allow the steam to escape while they are cooking.

9   Use the oven gloves to place the baking tray into the oven and bake for 15 to 25 minutes until golden and crisp.

10  Remove the tray from the oven using the oven gloves and set on a heat-resistant surface.

11  Lift the pies on to the cooling rack with the fish slice.

12  Allow your pies to cool before eating as the hot mincemeat could burn your mouth. Eat warm or cold. These pies are so good it is not difficult to eat twelve between Christmas Day and Twelfth Night – in fact it is tempting to eat them as soon as you make them!

## Whatever Happened to Plum Porridge?

Many hundreds of years ago, during feudal times, the wealthier folk made a sort of sweet fruity pudding-like dish called 'Plum Porridge' to eat on Christmas Day. However, as time passed (and certainly by the eighteenth century) this custom gave way to the making of Clootie Dumplings (the recipe is on the next page) and Plum Pudding instead. Silver baubles were often hidden in the puddings to bring luck to those who found one in their portion.

Try a few old traditional favourites on your Yule Table this year !

# Clootie Dumpling

*This pudding is boiled in a pudding cloth called a 'cloot' which is why it is called a 'Clootie Dumpling'. A Clootie Dumpling was a very special treat and was only made on special occasions like Christmas and New Year. Sometimes silver coins were hidden in the dumpling as a surprise.*

Adv

Serves 8

4 hrs

Cook ♒

Hob ◎

## HAVE READY

| | |
|---|---|
| 50g (2oz) vegetarian suet | 1 pint pudding basin |
| 110g (4oz) breadcrumbs | large soup pot + lid |
| 175g (6oz) flour | mixing bowl |
| 110g (4oz) raisins | measuring scales or spoons |
| 50g (2oz) soft brown sugar | lemon squeezer |
| 50g (2oz) currants | grater |
| 4 tablespoons apple juice | aluminium foil |
| 1 tablespoon black treacle | string or strong elastic band |
| 2 teaspoons baking powder | fancy dinner plate to serve |
| 1 level teaspoon mixed spice | chopping board |
| 1 teaspoon sunflower oil | sharp knife |
| grated rind and juice of 1 lemon | wooden spoon |
| pinch of salt | teaspoon |
| | sprig of holly (optional) |
| | kitchen towel |
| | oven gloves |

## TO MAKE

1 Put the pan on the hob and carefully pour in 3 pints of water. Turn the heat to medium and put the lid on the pan.

2 Grate the rind from the lemon (see page 13). Place the lemon on the chopping board and cut it in half with the sharp knife. Use the lemon squeezer (manual or electric) to squeeze out all the juice. Throw away the skin and pips, and pour the juice into the mixing bowl.

3 Put all the ingredients – apart from the sunflower oil – into the mixing bowl and stir together using the wooden spoon.

4 Pour the teaspoon of sunflower oil into the pudding basin and use a piece of kitchen towel to rub the oil all round the inside of the basin. This will help stop the dumpling from sticking to the basin.

5 Scrape the mixture into the basin and then cover the basin with the foil (see page 12).

6 By this time the water in the pan should be boiling. Using the oven gloves carefully lift the lid, keeping your face away from the hot steam which will escape. Lay the lid on a heat-resistant surface. Carefully, using the oven gloves, lower the pudding into the pan.

7 Turn down the heat until the water is just moving in the pan. Put the lid back on and steam the pudding for 3 hours.

8 During the cooking time you will need to check the water in the pan every 30 minutes. Carefully lift the lid (remember to wear oven gloves) and add more hot water if the pan looks as if it is boiling dry – there should always be enough water to come a third of the way up the side of the pudding basin.

9 When the pudding has cooked turn off the heat. Use the oven gloves to remove the pan lid and lift the pudding out on to a heat-resistant surface. Leave to cool for a few minutes.

10 Still wearing the oven gloves, remove the foil. Lift it away from the side and keep your face well back from the burning steam.

11 Run the knife round the inside of the pudding basin to loosen the edges.

12 Now you are going to be very professional! Lay the dinner plate over the top of the pudding. Use the oven gloves to grip the plate and the top of the bowl and flip the pudding basin over so that now the pudding basin is on top of the plate. The pudding will drop out of the bowl on to the plate.

13 Carefully ease the bowl off the pudding and decorate the top with the sprig of holly.

14 Serve hot with (low-fat) custard or fromage frais. Clootie Dumpling can be made in advance and kept to eat on Christmas Day. It is easy to reheat – just pop it into the microwave for about 40 to 50 seconds on full power, or steam it again for about 1 hour if you do not have a microwave.

## The story of the 'cloot'

The 'cloot' or cloth in which the dumpling was going to be cooked had to be wrung out in boiling water, laid flat and coated with flour. Immediately, the pudding mixture was piled in the centre. Then the corners of the cloot were quickly scooped up and securely tied with string. The dumpling was placed on a plate in a large pan and covered in slowly boiling water. The lid was placed on the pan and the pudding was cooked very slowly for up to 3 hours!!!

# Winter Salad

*Many of the big houses and shooting lodges in Scotland had large walled gardens where they grew a huge variety of fruit and vegetables. It is interesting to know that before potatoes were introduced to Scotland in the late 1700s, these sheltered gardens were able to grow green beans, artichokes, celery, cauliflowers and even asparagus.*

## HAVE READY

| | |
|---|---|
| 1 cooked beetroot | grater |
| 1 eating apple | vegetable brush |
| 2 lettuce leaves | chopping board |
| 1 head of celery | sharp knife |
| 2 teaspoons of lemon juice | small bowls |
| | 2 dinner plates |
| | teaspoon |

## TO MAKE

1 Prepare the celery: remove the outer stalks and throw them away. Separate all the other stalks and scrub each one well under running cold water. Use the knife to cut off the leaves and stalk ends. Use the knife to pull down the stalk to remove any stringy pieces and throw all these away.

2 Place a stalk on the chopping board and cut or slice along the length. Cut across the slices to make small cubes. Put the cubes into a bowl. Do the same with the other stalks.

3 Place the cooked beetroot on to a plate and cut it in half. Cut each half into slices, then cut each slice into strips and then into cubes. Add these to the bowl of celery.

4 Peel and core the apple (see page 11).

5 Hold the grater in the empty bowl and grate the apple into the bowl. Stir in the lemon juice – this prevents the apple from turning brown.

6 Lay the lettuce leaves on the clean dinner plate.

7 Spoon the celery and beetroot mixture on to the lettuce.

8 Top the celery and beetroot mixture with a teaspoon of grated apple and serve. This makes a tasty light winter snack – try topping the salad with grated (half-fat) cheese and eat with crusty fresh bread and a glass of milk.

# Pickles, Chutneys, Sauces and Spreads

From the mid-seventeenth to mid-eighteenth century the traditional Highland dress was a linen shirt (woven from home-grown flax) and a woollen plaid held in place by a huge buckled belt. The plaid was an all-purpose garment woven from home-spun, home-dyed wool. The Gaelic name for it was *feileadh mor* meaning 'great wrap'. It could also be used as a blanket at night. To put on the plaid, the belt was placed on the ground and the plaid was laid length-wise over it. The highlander then lay down on it with the belt at waist level and fastened the belt round his waist before he stood up. By 1730 a new version of the *feileadh mor* came into use called *feileadh beg* meaning 'little wrap', this name became corrupted to *phillabeg*. In this style the plaid was effectively cut into two pieces, the smaller piece being made into a kilt, while the other piece was worn as a cloak over the kilt and linen shirt.

# Pickled Beetroot

After the defeat of Bonnie Prince Charlie and his army at the battle of Culloden in 1746, the English, under the command of the Duke of Cumberland, did their best to destroy the Scottish clans. An act, called the Dress Act of 1746, was passed which forbade the wearing of tartan. If you broke this law and wore tartan you could be put in prison for six months without bail and if caught a second time you could be banished from Scotland for 7 years!

Needs to soak
for 2 hrs

Store in a cool
place 7 days
before opening

3 hrs

Cook 〰

Hob ◎

**116**

## HAVE READY

6 whole beetroot

1 litre (1¾ pints)
white wine vinegar

12g (½oz) black
peppercorns

12g (½oz) whole
allspice

1 piece of cinnamon
stick about 2cm
(1 inch) long

2 teaspoons salt

large pan + lid

enamel pan + lid

4 jam jars + screw-top
lids (450g/1lb sized)

15cm (6 inch) square
of muslin or fine cloth

½ metre (19 inch)
piece of string

sticky labels

colander

chopping board

jug

ladle

draining spoon

teaspoon

plate

knife + fork

rubber gloves

oven gloves

## TO MAKE

1 Carefully wash the beetroot under cold running water taking care not to break the skin. If you break the skin the beetroot will bleed into the cooking water. Wear rubber gloves to prevent your hands turning pink!

2 Half fill the large pan with cold water. Add 1 tablespoon of salt and put the pan on a medium heat. Bring to the boil.

3 Wearing the oven gloves carefully lower the beetroot into the pan using the draining spoon.

4 Bring the pan back to the boil and then reduce the heat until it is just simmering. Put the lid on the pan and cook for 1 hour until the beetroot is tender.

5 While the beetroot is cooking, prepare the vinegar. Take the piece of muslin, lay it flat, put the spices in the middle, lift up the corners to make it into a little bag and then tie the string round the top to keep the spices securely inside.

6 Put the spice bag into the enamel pan and tie the long tail of string round the handle of the pan to make it easy to pull out the spice bag.

7   Add the salt and vinegar to the enamel pan, place it on a medium heat and bring to the boil. Boil for 2 minutes. Turn off the heat and leave for 2 hours to soak or infuse ('infuse' means the flavour of the spices will transfer into the liquid).

8   Place the colander and the chopping board beside the sink.

9   When the beetroot is ready, turn off the heat and use the oven gloves to carefully lift the pan into the sink. Remove the lid and run cold water into the pan for a few minutes until the water in the pan is cold. Pour out half the water and set the pan on the chopping board.

10   Put the colander in the sink and use the draining spoon to lift the beetroot out of the pan into the colander. Run water over the beetroot until the water runs clear. Turn off the tap and leave the beetroot to cool for 10 minutes.

11   While the beetroot is cooling, write the name and date on the labels.

12   Put on the rubber gloves (this will stop your hands turning pink) and use your fingers to gently remove the skin from the beetroot. Run cold water over the beetroot to help rinse the skins off. Leave the skins in the colander and put the skinned beetroot on to the plate. Throw away the skins.

13   Use the knife and fork to cut the beetroot into slices. Carefully – try to keep the slices whole – put the slices into the jam jars.

14   When the vinegar is ready ladle it into the jug and pour the vinegar over the beetroot until each jam jar is filled.

15   Screw on the lid tightly and stick the labels on the jars. Leave in a cool place for a week before you use the beetroot; it will keep in the jars in a cool place for up to 6 months.

# Rhubarb Chutney

In the 1700s the Scots thought that rhubarb was a miracle cure for everything from the common cold and sore throats to more serious illnesses. As a result, they grew huge fields of it and ate lots of rhubarb – with custard, in puddings, pies, jams and even made into chutney.

Adv

Makes 3–4 lbs of chutney

1 hour

Cook ≋

Hob ◎

E. Wok ○

E. Fry ❖

## HAVE READY

450g (1lb) rhubarb

450g (1lb) soft brown sugar

225g (8oz) sultanas

570ml (1 pint) vinegar

1 onion

1 teaspoon salt

1 teaspoon ground ginger

½ teaspoon cayenne pepper

large enamel pan

chopping board

sharp knife

4 jam jars + screw-top lids (450g/1lb sized)

sticky labels

tray

ladle

wooden spoon

teaspoon

oven gloves

## TO MAKE

1 Wash the rhubarb under cold running water and chop into pieces about 1cm (½ inch) long.

2 Peel and chop the onion (see page 9).

3 Put the rhubarb, onion, salt, ginger, sugar, cayenne and vinegar into the pan and stir well.

4 Put the pan on a medium heat and bring to the boil, stirring all the time.

5 Reduce the heat until the chutney is just simmering and cook for 40 minutes, stir occasionally to prevent sticking. Don't cook it too quickly or the bubbling chutney may splash over the cooker and worse – over you!

6 Turn off the heat and leave to cool. While the chutney is cooling, write the name and date on the labels.

7 Put the jars on the tray beside the cooker. Ladle the cooled chutney into the jars and screw on the lids. Stick the labels on the jars.

8 Store in a cool, dry place; the chutney will keep for up to 6 months.

# Apple Chutney

The many abbeys and monasteries in Scotland were run by monks, and they were probably the first to bring cultivated fruit trees to Scotland. They brought apple and pear trees from France and grew them in their large walled gardens. The excess fruit was preserved in different ways for food in the long, cold winter months. One of the more unusual recipes is for apple chutney – wonderful with salads and cheese – try some with a crisp Potato Pasty (see page 72).

## HAVE READY

675g (1½lb) apples

225g (8oz) soft brown sugar

25g (1oz) salt

25g (1oz) dried mustard

845ml (1½ pints) light malt vinegar

25g (1oz) ground ginger

350g (12oz) onions

225g (8oz) raisins

large enamel pan

wooden spoon

measuring jug

4 jam jars + screw-top lids (450g/1lb sized)

sticky labels

tray

teaspoon

ladle

chopping board

sharp knife

oven gloves

## TO MAKE

1 Peel, core and chop the apples (see page 11). Put them into the pan.

2 Peel and chop the onions (see page 9). Place them in the pan with the apples.

3 Add all the other ingredients and stir together with the wooden spoon.

4 Put the pan on a medium heat and bring to the boil, stirring all the time.

5 Reduce the heat until the chutney is just simmering and cook for 45 minutes, stirring occasionally to prevent the chutney from sticking to the pan. Cook the chutney very slowly otherwise it will splash up and may burn you.

6 Turn off the heat and leave the chutney to cool.

7 While the chutney is cooling, write the name and date on the labels.

8 Put the jars on the tray beside the cooker. Use the ladle to fill them with the cooled chutney. Don't forget to stick the labels on the jars.

9 Store in a cool place; the chutney will keep for up to 6 months.

Adv

Makes 2 to 3 pounds

2 hours

Cook ﷽

Hob ◉

E. Wok ◖

E. Fry ❖

# Parsley Butter

In eighteenth century Scotland it became very fashionable to wear 'the tartan'. Tartan was used to make many items of clothing – jackets, trousers, coats, tartan frocks for girls and tartan breeches for boys. Ladies who supported the Jacobite cause wore the white cockade or a tartan shawl. So tartan became a national symbol.

## HAVE READY

25g (1oz) soft butter or vegetarian margarine

1 tablespoon chopped fresh parsley

2 teaspoons lemon juice

pinch of cayenne pepper (optional)

pinch of salt

pinch of black pepper

mixing bowl

wooden spoon

tablespoon

teaspoon

saucer

## TO MAKE

1 Put all the ingredients into the bowl and beat together with the wooden spoon.

2 Spread on a saucer and chill in the fridge until firm.

3 Cut the Parsley Butter into pieces and serve on hot grilled vegetables. It will melt and give the food a lovely taste.

# Carrot Spread

It was not until the eighteenth century that particular tartans were worn to identify each clan.
Before this the clansman wore a sprig of the clan's chosen plant in his bonnet. For example, the
McKenzies wore holly, the Gordons wore ivy and the Campbells wore wild myrtle.
This recipe can be made without nuts – try adding raisins or
crushed dried banana instead.

Simple

Serves 2

5 mins

No cook ☒

## HAVE READY

I large carrot –
peeled

I tablespoon cream
cheese (low-fat)

I teaspoon chopped
nuts (optional)

I teaspoon olive oil

I teaspoon lemon
juice

salt + pepper

mixing bowl

grater

wooden spoon

tablespoon

teaspoon

## TO MAKE

1  Put the grater into the mixing bowl and grate the carrot.
Remove the grater.

2  Add all the other ingredients and beat well together with
the wooden spoon. Season with salt and pepper to your
taste.

3  Serve spread on toast, cracker biscuits, bannocks or make
into sandwiches. Makes a tasty dip with sticks of celery.

# Green Pea Sandwich Filling

*Highlanders began to wear the famous blue bonnet at the end of the sixteenth century. Prior to this they would charge bare-headed into battle with a large piece of the clan plant tied to a long pole which was carried in front of the clan.*

Simple

Serves 2

20 mins

Cook ≋

Hob ◎

E. Wok ◯

E. Fry ❖

## HAVE READY

450g (1lb) green peas

1 sprig of mint

1 teaspoon salt

1 dessertspoon mayonnaise (reduced fat)

boiling water

saucepan

colander

mixing bowl

dessertspoon

wooden spoon

potato masher

oven gloves

## TO MAKE

1 Put the peas, mint and salt into the saucepan and cover with boiling water.

2 Place on a medium heat and bring to the boil. Reduce the heat and simmer for 10 minutes.

3 Put the colander into the sink and, using the oven gloves, lift the pan and carefully pour the peas into it to drain. Keep your face well back so that the steam does not burn you.

4 Pour some cold water into the pan and put the peas back into the cold water to cool for 5 minutes.

5 Drain the peas again through the colander. Throw away the mint.

6 Put the peas into the mixing bowl, add the mayonnaise and mash together with the potato masher.

7 Dip in a teaspoon, taste the sandwich filling and add salt and pepper if you think it needs it. This simple, tasty spread is lovely on fresh brown bread and makes great sandwiches with sliced cucumber and crisp lettuce.

# Potted Cheese

*Wearing a sprig of the clan plant in their bonnet identified each clan member. However, the sprig soon wilted so, in time, the clan members began to wear a piece of ribbon called a 'cockade' instead. In the Jacobite rebellion of 1745 when Bonnie Prince Charlie tried to win back the throne of Scotland, the Highlanders (called 'Jacobites') supporting his cause wore a white cockade.*

Simple

Serves 6 to 8

10 mins

No cook ☒

## HAVE READY

225g (8oz) hard cheese (such as Cheddar, Edam, Cheshire)

50g (2oz) vegetarian margarine (low-fat)

2 tablespoons natural yoghurt or fromage frais (low-fat)

1 level teaspoon ready made mustard

salt + pepper

mixing bowl

plastic container + lid

sticky label

grater

wooden spoon

teaspoon

## TO MAKE

1 Put the grater into the bowl and grate the cheese. Remove the grater.

2 Add the margarine, and mustard and beat together with the wooden spoon, adding a little more yoghurt or fromage frais if the mixture is too stiff.

3 Dip in a teaspoon and taste a little of the mixture. Add salt and pepper if you think it needs it.

4 Spread on hot toast, on cracker biscuits, in bannocks or make a tasty sandwich with sliced fresh tomatoes and fresh brown bread. Put the spread into a sealed plastic container, write the name and date on the label and stick it on the lid. Your Potted Cheese will keep up to two weeks in the fridge.

# Bibliography

Bingham, Caroline, *Beyond the Highland Line* (Constable, London)

Fitzgibbon, Theodora, *Traditional Scottish Cookery* (Souvenir Press Ltd., London)

Holt, Geraldene, *The Cookery book of Lady Clark of Tillypronie* (Southover Press, 1994)

Letters from a Gentleman in the North of Scotland, Vol. II (Oliver & Boyd, Edinburgh)

MacLaren, Kate M., *Mrs MacLaren's Cookery Book* (Moray & Nairn Newspaper Co., 1938)

McNeill, Marian F., *The Scots Kitchen* (Mercat Press, Edinburgh)

Paterson, William, *Burts Letters from the North of Scotland* (Edinburgh)

Warren, Janet, *A Feast of Scotland* (Lomond Books)

WRI, Edinburgh, *Scottish WRI Cookery Book* (6th Edition, 1946)

# Index